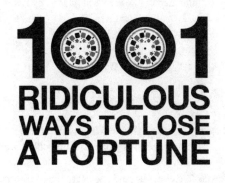

1001
RIDICULOUS
WAYS TO LOSE
A FORTUNE

First published in Great Britain in 2009 by Prion
an imprint of the
Carlton Publishing Group
20 Mortimer Street
London W1T 3JW

2 4 6 8 10 9 7 5 3 1

A catalogue record for this book is available from the British Library

ISBN 978-1-85375-742-6

Printed in the UK by CPI Mackays, Chatham, ME5 8TD

1001
RIDICULOUS
WAYS TO LOSE
A FORTUNE

The funniest, craziest and most downright idiotic
ways people have been parted from their cash!

Wayne Williams and Darren Allen

PRION

INTRODUCTION

Who'd have thought it? Apparently money does grow on trees (the roots of which are evil, and the branches of which are banks). Or so it would seem in these credit crunched times, where if you haven't got enough money, you can simply create it. Not by watering a tree, admittedly, but by just printing reams of the stuff.

Providing you're a central bank, of course. If we did that, it would be counterfeit and illegal. When they do it, it's called quantitative easing, or queasing for short. Presumably because you feel slightly sick when you think about all that bank bailout money that's flying around, which we'll have to pay for out of our pockets down the line.

But let's not start getting too depressed here. This book is about fiscal woes, for sure, but they're not your fiscal woes. Well, in truth the odd bank bailout is covered, as you could hardly write a definitive book about 1,001 ridiculous money losses without including the silly bankers. But there's so much more to the world of wealth wastage than them.

This book encompasses a vast tapestry of hilarious, daft and unbelievable tales. It's jam-packed with staggering business losses, erratic employees, gambling cock-ups, barking mad bets, ruinous real-estate deals, brazen scammers, squandered inheritances, expensive accidents and idiotic investments.

Within these pages, you'll find the story of the man who lost everything in a card game and upped the ante by throwing in his wife. The dotcom millionaire who had his £10 million mansion repossessed. The idiot who paid $2.5 million for a telephone number. The band who burned £1 million in cash. The golfer who gambled away over $50 million. The man who left a £180,000 violin on a train. The American financier who scammed to the tune of $50 billion. The poker player who lost $10,000, all because he refused to eat three olives.

Even if your bank balance is in the red, it can't be this bad. Go on and cheer yourself up by reading this collection of the most outrageous financial foolishness ever to be witnessed outside of an MP's expenses claim form.

Living on the Hedge

In 2007, an American hedge fund manager had a rather painful week in which he managed (which was his job) to lose $1.5 billion (which wasn't his job). His mistake? He bought corporate bonds on margin just before the credit markets crunched and their values tanked. I'm sure explaining this to his investors probably wasn't very easy, but it could have been worse. Maybe. I suppose if he had bet it all on weasel racing and on buying a packet of magic space beans from the spiral galaxy M95, for instance.

The Shitler Diaries

A German magazine believed it had netted the scoop of the century – an account of World War II written by Adolf Hitler himself. Hitler's lost diaries were allegedly discovered by a journalist in an East German hayloft and sold to the magazine for a reported nine million marks ($5 million). A further deal was done with a leading British newspaper, who paid $400,000 for the UK rights.

The problem was the diaries turned out to be fakes. Convincing though. Just take a look at this entry for September 1, 1939: "Dear Diary, Have persuaded Eva to wear a Nazi uniform in the bedroom tonight. Looking forward to annexing her Sudetenland later. Had Sauerkraut for dinner, again. Invaded Poland."

All You Need Is Glove

In 2007, a man wearing a single white glove on his right hand held up a bank. He managed to get away with a large amount of money, but dropped around three-quarters of his haul in a wooded area behind the bank. He also left the glove behind. Police initially suspected the bank robbery to be the work of Michael Jackson, but some children provided him with an alibi. The real suspect was quickly apprehended. There was no point in him trying to deny his guilt as the evidence was pretty damning. As Robert Palmer once almost sang, "Might as well face it, you're a dick with a glove."

Sinking Feeling

Matthew Webb was the first man ever to swim the English Channel in 1875. Subsequently, he wrote a book called *The Art of Swimming*. Evidently feeling pretty full of himself, eight years later he took on an extremely dangerous $10,000 bet to swim across the whirlpool at the bottom of Niagara Falls. He only made it halfway before he was sucked under to a watery grave. The obvious follow-up book, *The Art of Drowning*, was never published.

APPARENTLY 15,000 PILLOWS ARE WASHED DAILY AT THE MGM GRAND HOTEL AND CASINO, LAS VEGAS. PROBABLY TO GET ALL THOSE TEAR-STAINS OUT

Prize Plonkers

Plenty of people fall victim to prize draw scams, junk mail that arrives announcing that they've won some cash. Of course, you have to send off a cheque to cover a "processing fee" in order to release your windfall. The type of windfall you receive, sadly, is of the follow-through variety when you discover that someone has shat on you. A pensioner once spent an incredible £50,000 on attempting to claim prizes over her lifetime. A case of fool me once, shame on you... Fool me twice, shame on me... Fool me five thousand times, shame I forgot to go to the doctor's for my Alzheimer's test.

The Write Stuff

Writer Harold Robbins made a fortune from his racy novels, but claimed to have briefly been a millionaire in his youth too. After working in a grocery store for a short while, he had an idea and borrowed $800 which he used for speculating on crop futures. He was clearly brilliant at predicting which crops would meet tall, dark handsome strangers or get a promotion at work, as it reportedly netted him a million by the time he was 20 (in 1936). He later lost the lot by gambling on the future price of sugar (not sure if his fortune went in one lump, or two).

BEFORE 1996, BETTING SHOPS IN THE UK WEREN'T ALLOWED TO HAVE FRUIT MACHINES ON THE PREMISES - IN CASE IT ENCOURAGED GAMBLING

To Dye For

A bank robber had an accident in his pants as he fled the scene. A dye pack (hidden in the money he'd stolen and shoved down the waistband of his trousers) exploded, burning his crotch and showering him in a cloud of scarlet. The one-man Red Arrows display team dropped the money and stripped to his boxer shorts. Presumably in a rather addle-brained attempt to look less conspicuous. He was later caught red handed. And indeed red bollocked.

Honest Herrmann

In 1903, a cashier called Herrmann walked into the middle of a board meeting at the bank where he worked, and calmly told the directors he'd stolen $70,000. When asked why, he explained it was because they hadn't made him a director and this was his way of getting back at them. To be honest, pilfering a large sum of money from the bank sounds more like he was trying to show them all how good he'd be at the job. He eventually returned most of it, in exchange for a small sum and a lifetime pension. Which is different from today's bankers who would have kept it all and been given several lifetime's pensions and a golden handshake.

Body Blag

A deputy coroner pleaded guilty to stealing hundreds of dollars worth of gift cards from a dead person. The woman, from one of the southern U.S. states, was ordered to pay the money back and an extra $5,000 in fines. Which just goes to prove that old saying: Don't loot a gift corpse in the south.

Rotten Apple

A man who bought a $1,000 iPhone application called I Am Rich from the Apple Store later admitted he did so by accident. He must have been after I Am Stupid instead.

Stately Repo

A stately home in Scotland has been repossessed according to the BBC. It was originally on sale for the hefty price of £4.5 million back in 2003, but the owner eventually ran out of the financial wherewithal to keep it on when it failed to sell. He should have watched some House Doctor or Changing Rooms. A lick of magnolia here, one feature wallpaper wall there, a few strategically placed white scatter cushions and he'd have flogged it off no problems.

Suit You Sir

An anonymous buyer is said to have paid £70,000 for a suit from a London designer. It's made with extremely rare wool, gold thread, and a diamond laden button. The sort of suit that screams out "mug me" in more ways than one.

Spunky Woman

A twenty-something woman was alleged to have worked an Internet scam in 2007, conning a number of couples into believing she would be their surrogate mother. With nothing more than a web site, a simple promise and possibly a photo of a turkey baster, she milked the unsuspecting clients out of around $14,000 and several vials of sperm. Although perhaps milked is the wrong word to use.

Burning Ambition

The KLF were a big pop/dance act, and back in the early nineties they enjoyed considerable success. After the band was spent, they formed an "art duo" called the K Foundation. And they took £1 million that they'd earned from their music out to Jura, a small Scottish island, and they burnt it. Why? Well, Jura has only one small shop, there's sod all to spend money on, and it's freezing cold. Or it could have been some grand artistic and political statement, but quite frankly the former idea is less stupid.

THE FIRST MEMBERS OF GAMBLERS ANONYMOUS PLACED BETS ON HOW SUCCESSFUL IT WOULD BE

Unlucky Heather

The *Sunday Times* Rich List estimated Sir Paul McCartney lost around £60 million of his sizeable fortune in 2009. To be expected really, seeing as he had to get rid of some dead wood the previous year (surprising how many spare legs his ex-wife had). The divorce was costly, but it could have been much worse for Sir Paul. He could have changed his mind and stayed married to Heather.

Merry Merrill

Finance management firm Merrill Lynch did not have a good 2008. In trouble, they were bought up by the Bank of America, and according to *The Times* suffered a loss of $27 billion in value due to poor and/or risky investments. The ex-CEO is also alleged to have spent $35,000 on an office toilet. Presumably made of gold and platinum with inset emeralds. Or perhaps it was just really large. I guess they needed somewhere substantial to flush away all that money.

Out Of Luck

Former Australian media tycoon Kerry Packer, who died in 2005, was a canny businessman, and one of the most powerful men in the country. Stories about his gambling are legendary. One report claimed that he lost £13 million in three days of baccarat in Las Vegas. It's also rumoured he once tipped a waitress a house. No idea how she got that home in her handbag.

IN POKER, A HAND OF FOUR KINGS IS NICKNAMED THE FOUR HORSEMEN

Betting Revelation

Out of all the wagers in this book, a London man didn't make the biggest (the amount isn't actually specified), but he made possibly the stupidest. He was evidently tempted to place it because of the 1,000,000 to 1 odds he was given. So what was it? That he could go on a tube train and strike up a friendly conversation with a random stranger?

No. It was even more inconceivable than that. He bet that the world would end before the year 2000. The massively obvious question being, exactly how did he plan to pick up his winnings if it did? Maybe he'd read a bit of the Bible the rest of us missed... "And yay, also on the fourth day God created Ladbrokes, on the fifth cloud from the left behind the pearly gates (you can't miss it, right next to KFC)."

Lost Fortune

If you're going to win the lottery, make sure that you don't use Hurley's winning numbers from the TV series *Lost*. If they did come up as the jackpot, you'd be sharing your winnings with the loads of other people who imitate the famous digits. This almost happened in the Irish national lottery in 2005, when 4, 8, 15,16, 23 and 24 were drawn (identical but for the last number which was reversed, in Lost it's 42). Apparently 300 people matched 5 numbers, presumably all Lost viewers, and they only won 300 Euro apiece.

Big Ticket

In 2003, a Finnish millionaire was penalised with what must surely be the most expensive speeding ticket ever. According to the BBC, he was doing 80Km/h in a 40Km/h limit area, and was fined £116,000 by the authorities. The fine was that large because in Finland it's proportionate to your income. Good news for tramps who can find big enough downhill runs to get up speed in their shopping trolleys.

Not So Beneficial

According to one newspaper report, in 2006-7 the UK government recovered £22 million back from benefit fraudsters. Unfortunately it's alleged they spent over £150 million on the investigations. Whoops. You could give them the benefit of the doubt, only you'd probably never see it again.

Charity Ends Up at Home

A charity lost £150,000 to a finance executive who confessed to stealing the money by writing cheques and covering his trail with false invoices. Apparently he spent the ill-gotten gains on cars, bikes and flying lessons of all things. Guess he really did yearn to be a high-flier.

IT'S THOUGHT THAT IT WOULD TAKE AROUND 330 YEARS TO SLEEP A NIGHT IN EVERY HOTEL ROOM IN LAS VEGAS

Card Partner

A Russian gambler raised the stakes when he ended up running low on cash in a card game. He put his wife into the pot, and a fellow gambler ended up winning the hand. Not just the hand, in fact, but her hand in marriage too, as she was so mad with her husband when she found out about the bet that she actually left him and settled down with the guy who won her. Possibly the first time in history that the winner has taken home the booby prize.

Utter Madness

Madness singer Suggs probably went more than mad when he lost a bet to DJ Christian O'Connell over who could drink the most Guinness. The forfeit was that Christian got to plunge the star's prize Rolls Royce into a swimming pool. An extremely expensive car wash, no doubt.

Copper Load of This

In 1996, the Japanese trading house Sumitomo Corporation disclosed mammoth losses of $2.6 billion in the copper market. Heavy metal losses indeed. The company blamed unauthorised actions by one of its traders known as "Mr Copper". Although they probably called him something else after that episode.

Football Crazy #1

In 2006, a scandal hit the Vietnamese government when the equivalent of millions of dollars was reported to have been embezzled from aid funds. These huge quantities of Vietnamese Dong were blown on gambling, primarily on football matches. Their mothers should have warned them, you've got to be careful about what you do with your Dong.

On the Edsel

The much hyped Ford Edsel car of the late 1950s failed to strike a chord with the American public, many of whom thought the shape in the middle of the front grille looked like a toilet seat. Profits certainly went down the pan, with varying sources estimating Ford's losses at around $250-350 million.

Rubber Cheque

A famous casino was down over £6 million after a high-rolling man wrote two massive cheques for gambling chips which he spent on roulette. The cheques later bounced. When he returned to the casino, what's the bettering the only chips they were prepared to sell him came in a polystyrene tray with a wooden fork?

UFOols

A Taiwanese businesswoman and her husband gave a man they didn't know all of their savings after he told them he had come from outer space to save the planet and could, for a fee, sort them out a lift in his flying saucer. He showed them some photos of mountains with sun glare (aka alien energy) and told her husband, who suffered from headaches, the aliens could fix him right up. Fully convinced, they handed over $300,000. Oddly enough, the spaceship never came to collect them. The couple possibly had the last laugh though – it's highly unlikely that dollars were legal tender on the extra-terrestrial's home world.

Dear Beer

A man from New Zealand had a beer in a bar, signed off the credit card slip, and later discovered he had paid NZD$2,500 for the drink. He claimed that staff must have tampered with the bill, and swore that when he ratified it the amount read $2.50. Unfortunately for him, his card company didn't credit his story, or his account, and he ended up paying for probably the most expensive draught beer in history. One that makes Stella Artois look unassumingly cheap in comparison.

Lay Down

A lay preacher was jailed for a £51 million "carousel fraud" in 2007. Which has nothing to do with charging for goes on an imaginary merry-go-round. It's actually a scheme whereby HM Revenue and Customs is cheated out of VAT by disappearing companies.

Khashoggi Lolly

In 1982, when Soraya Khashoggi got divorced from her husband, the Saudi businessman Adnan Khashoggi, he had to pay up a princely sum. The exact figure varies considerably from source to source, but one estimate alleged that she received something in the region of $800 million. Never mind getting over a failed relationship by tucking into a tub of ice cream; with that amount of dosh she could afford to buy up Ben and Jerry's and employ a team of women to eat their way through the entire stock on her behalf.

Poker Mania

A travel agent was sent to jail for stealing some $50,000 from her employer in Australia. She took the money over a period of 18 months to feed her addiction to poker gaming machines, Australia's take on fruit/slot machines. They're known as "pokies", and are very popular down under. Though the only thing poky about where this woman went was her cell.

THE LEAST OFTEN PICKED UK LOTTERY NUMBERS ARE 13, 16, 20, 21, 36 AND 41

Hedge Bet #1

In 2006, hedge fund Amaranth Advisors' speculation on the natural gas futures market went badly awry. It suffered losses to the tune of $6 billion in September, causing the fund to collapse. Which just goes to prove, the only safe bet on gas is that it'll peak after you've had a vindaloo.

Basketball Case

In 2008, the LA Lakers made the NBA finals, and it's rumoured that a poker professional wagered a seven figure sum on his team. The Lakers lost, which presumably led to a seven figure stream of swear words.

Paget from the History Books

Edward Paget was an amateur jockey and stockbroker (which is perhaps the literal definition of a turf accountant). In 1932 he placed a £1 bet at vast odds of 4,000 to 1 on the spring double – the Lincolnshire Handicap and Grand National. His first race pick came in the winner, and he was riding the second horse in the National himself. He was just pipped at the post after a lengthy battle for the lead, failing to scoop the £4,000. Unlike most punters who narrowly miss out on a massive jackpot, he only had himself to blame. Well, himself and the horse. Rumours that the next day at work he invested heavily in glue factory shares are entirely unsubstantiated.

AN ESTIMATED 3% OF THE UK POPULATION STILL DOES THE FOOTBALL POOLS

Trashing the Ivories

A removal firm who were transporting a £45,000 piano to a festival looked on in horror as it fell off the tail lift of the van into a ditch, hitting a very flat note. Presumably that's another fine mess they got themselves into.

Shoe Fetish

Imelda Marcos, the former First Lady of the Philippines, infamously spent money on footwear. Lots of money. Over the years she must have footed a considerable bill for her reputed 3,000 strong collection of expensive shoes. Still, she was probably glad of them when she fled the country in 1986 during the revolution – bet she had a bloody good pair of trainers to leg it in.

Domain Pain

If you've ever set up your own web site, you'll realize you have to stump up a bit of money to buy the domain name. But consider the buyers of sex.com, an understandably popular domain rumoured to have sold for around $10-12 million. Which would make it the most expensive domain ever. Sex sells, and no doubt sex.com really sells, but still, who'd ever have thought that six little letters would be so costly?

Oven Tit

An English barman who was left to cash up put the pub's takings (£1,000) in an oven for safe keeping (apparently). Trouble was the oven was still on, which he realized soon after when he smelled burning. Guess it's money the taxman won't get, although it's one extreme way of cooking the books.

Soaring Eagles

One story about a famous rock group claims that they played a private party at which they only performed one tune, a classic about a hotel. And it's alleged they charged $6 million for the privilege. According to the song the hotel is a lovely place, but $6 million for a five-minute stay seems a bit steep even by a billionaire's inflated standards.

Not a Truffling Amount

How much would you pay for a giant 1.5 kilogram mushroom? Probably not $330,000 at a guess. But that's the amount a billionaire entrepreneur handed over for a big lump of fungus in 2007. Admittedly it was a white truffle, the most expensive mushroom in the world, but even so. He didn't say what he planned to do with it, perhaps preferring to keep his reporters, like his mushrooms, in the dark.

Gold Vibrations

The luxury end of the sex toy market sees some pretty outrageous money wastage. Like an 18-carat gold plated vibrator which can get well-off folk's rocks off for a thousand bucks. $1,000 for a gold-finger seems a bit much, especially when there are some real budget options out there. The traditional wine bottle neck for example, or perhaps a simple, one carrot, carrot.

Dial-a-Devil

In 2006, an anonymous bidder paid out over $2.5 million for a telephone number. It was: 666-6666. The phone number of the beast, presumably. It was certainly a hellishly expensive collection of digits.

Poker Broke

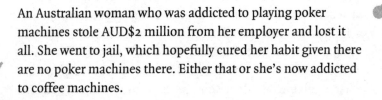

An Australian woman who was addicted to playing poker machines stole AUD$2 million from her employer and lost it all. She went to jail, which hopefully cured her habit given there are no poker machines there. Either that or she's now addicted to coffee machines.

ONLY TWO GREY HORSES HAVE EVER BEEN VICTORIOUS IN THE GRAND NATIONAL

Start Spreading the Bill

In 1897, Mr and Mrs Bradley-Martin held a costume ball in a New York hotel, which they billed as the greatest party in the history of the city. It was a sheer display of excessive affluence. The interior of the hotel was apparently transformed into a replica of Versailles, with thousands of roses and orchids adorning the place, rich tapestries hanging on the walls, rare truffles served as food and so on.

The final cost of the ball was estimated to be a heart-stopping $370,000, an absolute fortune at the time. The icing on the cake was generally deemed such a vulgar display of wealth that apparently the authorities subsequently raised the couple's taxes. Now that's what you call a real ball-ache.

Power Down

In February 1998, a power cut hit Auckland in New Zealand, but this was no normal outage. It lasted for many weeks, and even though some alternative power sources were brought in (generators and suchlike) as temporary measures, it still caused chaos and cost the capital's businesses a fortune. Estimates put the fiscal damage at something like $150 million. That's a hell of a lot of candles.

Key Mistake

Slips on a computer keyboard can be pretty costly, as one trader at an investment bank showed in 2005. According to reports at the time, he meant to sell a basket of £3 million worth of FTSE 100 stocks, but hit the wrong keys and actually sold £300 million, a move that caused a substantial plunge in the market. A final zero may well have been added after the event, by the boss on his payslip.

Landed In It

An American couple got more than they bargained for when they cashed in a free trip to a casino – with spending money – that they received in the mail. Of course, when they arrived they had to look at a plot of land first, in a soon-to-be ski resort, no less. Talked into it by the salesman they invested the $10,000 savings they had. And guess what? There was no ski resort coming. The land couldn't be developed. To make matters worse, they had to continue to pay taxes on the plot as well, being unable to sell it off. All in all, it was snow joke.

Car Cash

During a high speed police pursuit in an American city, two suspected drug dealers tried to dispose of their ill-gotten gains by chucking $17,000 (in $20 and $100 bills) out of the car window onto the freeway behind. That really is what you call just throwing money away.

Bum Steer

In 1966, an elderly widow who had spent much of her life savings on learning to drive decided to buy a car. She handed over the last of her cash to pay for the vehicle and prepared to hit the road. It was only then that she discovered despite years of expensive lessons that she couldn't actually drive. The woman's instructor, who had only ever allowed her to go on straight roads, had secretly been using dual controls the whole time.

A Clever Scheme

Charles Ponzi amassed a fortune in the early twentieth century by means of a scam that came to be known as the Ponzi scheme. He purchased postal coupons cheaply abroad and traded them in for more expensive U.S. stamps, which he then sold for a profit. He persuaded friends to put money into his scheme and paid them huge dividends. Suddenly everyone wanted to be involved. People who invested initially, re-invested their returns. He was soon making millions. There was just one problem. The money he was paying to his early backers was coming from his later ones. He was taking from Peter to pay Paul. Eventually the scheme, with no foundations at all, came crashing down like a tsunami, wiping out countless investors and six banks. Ponzi was arrested and spent much of his life in prison until he died in 1949. Thirty years later, Henry Winkler did not recreate his life in the popular TV show *Happy Days*.

Bank On It

A bank manager stole nearly £60,000 from his branch by opening fake accounts in existing customers' names, and then gambled the lot away at a rate of nearly £750 per day. The judge said: "I can't imagine a more selfish or worthless use of funds" before sentencing him to two years in prison. The defendant was clearly distraught. He had two grand riding on getting 18 months.

Poker Farce

Actor Herbert Ransom was a member of a poker club, and apparently a poor player who was unable to control his excitement when he was dealt a good hand. (Obviously he wasn't that great an actor, either). His lamentably bad poker face doubtless lost him a lot of money. And it was evidently the source of many jokes at the club, with one member proposing a new rule: "Anyone looking at Ransom's face is cheating."

Mistress Distress

Madame de Montespan, mistress of Louis XIV of France, was apparently a bit of a gambler. She reputedly lost four million francs in one single half-hour gambling session. Her nickname was supposedly Quanto, which translates to "How much." Presumably because the King was always asking her how much she'd lost this time.

THE BEST POKER HAND IS "A-K-Q-J-10" OF THE SAME SUIT (A ROYAL FLUSH)

No Expenses Spared

In May 2009, the Labour Care Services Minister and MP for Corby and East Northants, Phil Hope, asserted that he had kept to the rules of MP expenses. However, he pledged to repay the £41,000 used to furnish and refurbish his second home because he felt stories surrounding the episode had caused a serious blow to his integrity with voters. According to *The Daily Telegraph*, he had claimed for a barbecue (one of life's essentials), a washing machine and a wardrobe.

Camel Piss

In 1996, a UK brewery produced Tutankhamen Ale, which was a limited edition beer as they only had enough ingredients (recovered by archaeologists from the Sun Temple of Queen Nefertiti) to produce 1,000 bottles. The first bottle sold for £5,000, which is one ludicrously expensive beer. Even more so when you consider that the rest went for more like a few hundred pounds. Anyone supping a bottle of Tutankhamen Ale would, of course, be compelled to do one thing: Drink like an Egyptian.

Dog Pays

A couple from America paid out a whopping $155,000 for a dog. A price that makes even Paris Hilton's Chihuahua look cheap (perish the thought). But what they actually paid for was a cloned puppy of their deceased dog, which apparently they had taken samples from some years back. (Samples of what exactly isn't clear, but best not to think about it). Obviously the puppy isn't the only thing that's barking.

Two Go Bad In Dorset

In late 2008, the spectre of repossession reached the prestigious real-estate peninsula of Sandbanks in Dorset, one of the most expensive places to live in the world. A pair of million pound plus homes were reportedly repossessed, the first to have been seized back since the last major property dive of the 1990s. Although living on the sands, presumably the owners are used to life being a beach.

Bacca-Rats #1

The Sands Hotel in Las Vegas was apparently the first casino to open a baccarat pit back in 1959. The first game attracted plenty of high-rollers, but it was rather a disaster for the casino, which allegedly lost some $250,000 on the night. Perhaps they focused on some slightly lower rollers for the rest of the week.

THE LARGEST CASINO IN THE WORLD IS THE VENETIAN IN MACAU, WHICH COVERS OVER 550,000 SQUARE FEET

Get Beal

One self-made billionaire is famous for playing high stakes poker against the pros. He has won some games and lost some, but one of his most spectacular defeats came in 2006 when he is alleged to have dropped over $16 million in the space of just a few days. Not so much a case of Texas Hold 'Em, as Texas Hold Up.

Bingo Flings

A bingo addict from Canada who gambled away her life savings playing the game decided she would sue the company for $70,000. They settled out of court for an undisclosed amount, but apparently the money is going to a third party to dole it out to her in small chunks, as the woman doesn't trust herself to look after it all without hearing the call of the bingo again. Sounds like she's finally recovering some financial sanity after the many years she's bingo-ing mad.

Millionaire's Short of Bread

A dotcom millionaire had his London mansion repossessed in 2008. According to the Council of Mortgage Lenders' records, the posh pad is the most expensive to have been repossessed in British history, being put up for sale for a record-breaking £10 million. Presumably that includes carpets and curtains.

THE VENETIAN CASINO IN MACAU HAS 3,400 SLOT MACHINES, 800 GAMING TABLES, AND A 15,000 SEAT ARENA

Not So Funny Money

A Chinese worker discovered his life savings (2,600 yuan, around $380) had been switched for counterfeit notes while he was visiting a prostitute. Feeling doubly f**ked, he went to the police but when they were too slow to react, he spent his remaining three yuan on a large knife and went off in search of the person who had taken his money. With no actual leads, he resorted to knifing people indiscriminately, killing one and injuring nine. The police didn't say if he'd had anal sex with the prostitute but it's a possibility seeing he was a shit stabber.

Microscam

An American man placed an advert for "the next Microsoft" on a reputable financial website. Anyone clicking the ad was taken to the company's site which detailed an impressive (and entirely fictional) cutting-edge product. They were then given the chance to invest online. He made $190,000 in three months from the scam, including $10,000 wired over from an eager investor in Hong Kong. "The next Bill Gates" was eventually arrested but his victims never got their money back.

Le Coq Up

A trader at a French bank was accused by his employers of unauthorized transactions which led to losses of almost 5 billion Euro in January 2008. The trader claims that his superiors were aware of his actions. The investigation is ongoing, but either way it's a lot of money to lose. A sort of reverse Euromillions.

Lord Of The Lies

Retired army captain Arthur Lipscombe couldn't have been happier when his daughter married into nobility. Lord Jefrey Jess le Vance de Roath was the illegitimate son of Lord Sinclair of Cleve and Duchess Katrina de Roath, and a part-time British Secret Service agent. He was, in every way, the ideal son-in-law. Except perhaps for the bit where he turned out to be a fraud (called Burke) who'd "borrowed" and spent £4,000 of his father-in-law's savings...

Counter Fit

When police arrested a suspected terrorist at Durham Tees Valley Airport in 2008 they were rather surprised to discover he was carrying counterfeit cheques and bank drafts worth over £69 million. He claimed he was looking after them for a friend and had no intention of trying to cash the fakes. Hoping to avoid getting into trouble (which failed) he tore them all up on the spot. A ripping yarn if ever there was one.

Vegas Vagrant

A Las Vegas man was severely out of luck, homeless and down to his last $400 from the social security. So naturally he headed down to the casino and put it on blackjack. Incredibly, he managed to turn it into $1 million, and then perhaps more predictably, he carried on playing and lost the lot. Including his original $400. Still, bet it was a hell of a tale to tell while gathered around the rusty-oil-barrel fires that night.

Down Under

The company secretary of an Australian firm is alleged to have funnelled out £8 million from its funds and gambled it away. According to the court reports he had a weakness for slow horses. Not to mention fast money with an affinity for pouring down plugholes.

A Bad Habit

Richard John Dugdale moved to France in the mid-nineteenth century and invested the money he'd made from a successful manufacturing business into his own newspaper, the Paris Sun. The paper made him a small fortune but then the government fined him for publishing an unflattering article, his finances took a further battering in the French Revolution of 1848 and a Benedictine monk emptied his bank account using forged papers. He tried to make light of the last one but it was hardly much ado abbot nothing.

Baking a Loss

British baking clan the Warburton family would probably have expected their fortune to rise like their products in 2009, but according to The *Sunday Times* Rich List they instead lost around £100 million. That's a lot of bread to part with. They're still worth £330 million though, so it's not like they knead the dough.

Night Mayor

An ex-mayor was jailed for 12 months for stealing money to fund her gambling addiction in 2009. She funnelled away over £30,000 from a social club, and lost it all gambling online. According to newspaper reports she had also taken money previous to this, and had forged her husband's signature on a mortgage document to pay it back. Who said that in gambling the house never pays out?

Million Mum

An American single mum who bagged $1 million on the lottery has since bemoaned the depressing reality of her jackpot. She used the money to buy a home, go on some holidays, and open her dream business, a restaurant. Four years after her win, however, she was forced to close the restaurant, and had no savings left. Or to put it another way, if the lottery win was a meal ticket, the final course was her money "desserting."

Online Shopping

A couple who adopted twin baby girls over the Internet ended up losing their savings and their home. After spending a month in America, and an estimated £30,000 on bringing the girls over to the UK (Fedex would have been cheaper), they found themselves and their dubious adoption method front page news. The girls were taken from them and returned to the States, leading to a costly legal fight which the couple lost. Maybe stick to buying DVDs online next time.

Keepy Uppy

Two women bet a Russian mechanic $5,000 that he wouldn't be able to keep going non-stop through an all day sex session with them. Probably about the going rate down a brothel for that sort of thing anyway, so he doubtless figured he didn't have much to lose. How wrong he was, because apparently he was so serious about winning he reportedly downed an entire bottle of Viagra. Needless to say he remained upright throughout the 12-hour marathon, and was even stiffer at the end of it. Mainly because he died of a heart attack. Still, at least he went out with a bang. A gang bang, in fact.

Flying Dangerously

A finance officer who felt aggrieved when he wasn't awarded a bonus for saving his airline employers $6 million in costs set up his own fake firm and began paying himself with company money. He managed to steal £2 million before he was caught and jailed for four years. It was plane crazy to think he'd get away with it.

Mission Kim-Possible

Actress Kim Basinger liked the town of Braselton, Georgia so much she bought it (along with a group of investors) for $20 million. Unfortunately, a few years later she was sued for backing out of the film *Boxing Helena* and ordered to pay $8.1 million in damages – way more than the film made at the box office. Although this ruling was eventually overturned she was forced to file for bankruptcy and sell her share of the town for just $1 million. Still, who needs a celebrity endorsement anyway? Brasthingie, Wotsit managed just fine without her.

Casino Mug

A man from Vienna lost thousands at a casino, and was afraid to break the news to his wife. So he broke his own nose instead, and apparently his jaw and an arm, using a hefty iron bar for good measure. All so he could tell her he'd been robbed of the money rather than the truth. He had to admit himself to hospital later, where hopefully he realized that you should never beat yourself up over your losses.

THE FIRST OFFICIAL GRAND NATIONAL WAS WON BY A HORSE CALLED LOTTERY IN 1839

Bank Unbalance

An employee at a merchant bank allegedly salted away £460,000 in a period of five months, which she then gambled and lost on the horses and other sports bets at up to £10,000 a pop. She was ordered to attend Gamblers Anonymous meetings for two years, where apparently she made good progress and beat her addiction. Mind you, it shouldn't have been too hard to persuade her to go, most bankers want to remain anonymous these days.

No Place Like Rome

Roman Emperor Caligula was a notoriously cruel tyrant of a ruler, who enjoyed gambling and horse racing. He built his own race track, splashed out money on horses, and it's rumoured he used to poison his rival's steeds to ensure victory. He was also a big dice player, often betting huge sums and losing cash hand-over-iron-fist. He had a simple solution to recoup his gambling pot, however; he'd just go out, nick a noble's estate and execute them. Perhaps they were burned at the stake (and their money was burned through as a stake).

Slim Pickings

One poker pro is said to have once beat a famous American country singer to the tune of $300,000. At dominoes, of all things. A loss that must have really knocked the spots off the singer. Perhaps the gambler should have changed his poker nickname to "Dominator."

Cards and Punishment

Russian author Dostoyevsky wrote a staggering amount. Of IOUs, when he'd lost a lot of money betting, by all accounts. After being knocked hard by deaths in his family in the 1860s, he sank into depression and debt, and spent time in gambling dens. According to one source, one of his novels was completed in a big hurry, as he desperately needed the advance after a particularly bad gambling session had left him broke.

Boner Part

Napoleon made a rather hasty decision back at the beginning of the nineteenth century, when the French empire was being stretched, not least by a revolt in Haiti. He decided to get rid of Louisiana by selling it to the United States in short order (mind you, arguably everything he did was a short order). He got around $15 million for the land. Today it's worth a vast amount more than that, even with his sale price adjusted for inflation (about $15 billion, give or take).

Fourteen Big Ones

In 1993, a South Korean businessman apparently lost $14 million playing the roulette wheel in a London casino. Russian roulette might be more dangerous, but at least it's not nearly as expensive as the South Korean variety.

Back to the Past

John DeLorean quit a promising career at General Motors in 1973 to make his own car, which of course was the famous model as seen in the *Back to the Future* films. However, despite being backed by £85 million from the British government, the quirky DeLorean didn't fare so well in the real world. When it was launched in 1981 it allegedly suffered from some mechanical bugbears (probably trouble with the flux capacitor). Less than 9,000 were made before production ground to a halt. Still, those flip up doors were really cool. John was accused of dealing cocaine, and then acquitted in 1984 (he said it was entrapment) before eventually bankrupt in 1999.

Horsing About

An arab Sheikh reportedly paid £250,000 to fly 30 members of the Household Cavalry to the middle east, so they could perform their famous musical ride for him. A specially adapted Boeing 747 jet was used to transport the horses. It's not known if they flew business class or coach.

Telephone Fall

In 2008, the telephone technology tycoon Anil Ambani saw his personal fortune drop a reported $30 billion, after stock in his telecoms company fared badly following a deal falling through. A wake-up call that he could have done without. While it's Anil wind that blows, Ambani is not exactly out on the streets with a tin cup and a banjo yet; just down to his last $12 billion.

Flat Fanatic

John Hampden was a firm believer that the Earth was flat, but in 1870 Alfred Wallace bet him £500 (£40,000 or so today) that he could prove it wasn't using a scientific test that measured the curvature of a canal's surface. Dopey John agreed to the wager, and unsurprisingly a third party appointed as a judge verified that Wallace's test did indeed show that the Earth curved away from the observation point.

Apparently Hampden still disputed the point, and proceeded to write offensive threatening letters. He is reputed to have written to Wallace's wife: "If your infernal thief of a husband is brought home some day on a hurdle, with every bone in his head smashed to a pulp, you will know the reason." Presumably because he had a nasty fall. Off the edge of the world.

Big Stakes

An English bond trader made a fortune in the 1980s. Money he regularly bet on the horses. He's alleged to have gambled away around £58 million in a period of three years, including a £1 million bet on a horse race. The filly he backed was called Below Zero, apparently, which is pretty much where his bank balance finished when he went bankrupt in 1992.

Jewel in the Clown

Gerald Ratner will always be associated with the gaffe he made while giving a speech to the Institute of Directors in 1991. Gerald, head of the thriving Ratners jewellers, thought he'd liven things up with a couple of gags. He reportedly joked that a sherry decanter they made was "total crap", and a pair of gold earrings were "cheaper than a prawn sandwich." But it all got rather more lively than he anticipated, as the press seized on his comments, and in the ensuing furore £500 million was wiped off the value of the company. He lost his job and £650,000 salary, and was doubtless left feeling a right pair of gold earrings himself.

Margaretta Time!

Margaretta Davis met the man of her dreams in 1939. Claus Spreckels was tall, handsome, and rich – the heir to a £6 million fortune. He promised he'd buy her a yacht, jewellery and beautiful clothes when they were betrothed, and they'd travel the world for their honeymoon. After a whirlwind romance they married and lived happily ever after – well up to the point when he told her he was actually Nathan Desmond, a penniless San Francisco salesman, and that the life of luxury she'd recently been living had been paid for with her own savings.

Strip-freeze

When an Internet gambling company organised an extreme poker tournament in the Arctic circle, it wasn't strip poker as such, but the contestants had the option of exchanging their thick Parkas to buy back lost chips. And with the temperature at a biting minus 23 degrees Celsius, the prospect of losing the coat off your back was no laughing matter. The eventual winner ended up in his T-shirt, and running laps around the table to try and keep his circulation going between hands. And between his legs, and everywhere else probably.

Fruit Loopy

A slot machine player at a casino in New Mexico couldn't believe his luck when he put in his nickel and scored a jackpot of $1.6 million. Unfortunately for him, he'd lost the million and a half almost as quickly as he'd won it, when the casino told him that it was a computer glitch and the machine's maximum payout was $2,500. According to the man they gave him $400 and some complimentary meals instead. And who said there's no such thing as a free lunch?

Student Debt

A drama student was offered a large overdraft by a bank keen on his business. He accepted, spent all the money on a holiday to Amsterdam, and then opened a new account with a different bank. When he ran out of money a second time, he opened two new accounts with two other banks. When his overdrafts became overdrawn he found he could keep spending by using his card for cashback from local shops. In a year the performance arts student managed to spend his way through £40,000 of bank money and was eventually forced to declare himself bankrupt. That's what you call making a crisis out of drama.

Oils Not Well

Stockbroker Dennis Banyard was determined to make his first million, a lot of money back in 1956. He had a foolproof plan, all he needed was the funds to put it into action. Fortunately his clients had the money, so he stole it from them. Believing Britain would take over the Suez Canal he bought up as many oil shares as he could get his hands on. When the canal was lost, oil prices plummeted and Banyard found himself losing his first £100,000 instead. His company collapsed and he went to jail for the fraud, no doubt feeling very Suezcidal about the whole affair.

Stern Admonishment #1

Things looked good for one property magnate back in the late 1960s and early 1970s. His company rode the property boom of the time and enjoyed large scale investments, but it all went pear-shaped when a banking crisis and then recession hit (sounds familiar). In 1974, he was declared bankrupt owing a reported £118 million (which is more like a billion in today's money). It was Britain's biggest bankruptcy at the time.

Russian-ish Roulette

The owner of a successful Greek car company is alleged to have lost around £8 million during a disastrous roulette session in 1994. I'd imagine his head was spinning as fast as the wheel by the end of that.

WITH FIVE CARDS DEALT IN POKER, THE PROBABILITY OF GETTING A FULL HOUSE IS 1 IN 700

Cooking The Books

One actor's half-brother was arrested in December 2008 and charged with embezzling millions while working as his brother's manager. He was accused of transferring money directly into his own account and forging a cheque worth $3 million. I'm trying to find a funny side to the story, but there isn't one. I'm thinking of the actor's comic movies though, not the embezzlement case.

The Waiting Game

In 1931, Rosamond Templeton (aged 85) won a big legal case over the site of the Haifa railway station in Palestine. It was agreed that the land it was built on was owned by her first husband, Laurence Oliphant, and she received an £18,000 payment for the rights to it. She promptly gave the majority of it away. The case took 47 years to settle, which is a ridiculously long time, but fortunately an Oliphant never forgets.

High Wire

An American man used his mobile phone's wireless net connection to download a film to his laptop when away in Mexico, and was charged $62,000 for the privilege. Apparently this was later reduced to $17,000, but even by contemporary cinema ticket and snack prices, that's one expensive movie. The film in question was WALL-E, rather appropriately.

IN THE UK IN 2008, CITIZENS ADVICE BUREAUX HAD TO DEAL WITH NEARLY 5,000 DEBT PROBLEMS DAILY

Titanic Misjudgement

20th Century Fox made what turned out to be a costly error when it came to the blockbuster *Titanic*. As the film's production costs spiralled, the company sought a partner and sold half of the rights to Paramount for $60 million. Given that the movie went on to be the most successful ever, grossing an estimated $600 million in the U.S. ($1.8 billion worldwide), Paramount has certainly recouped its original investment many times over. And Fox is probably feeling none too cunning regarding that decision.

Raking It In

Legend has it that in the 1930s a golfer by the name of LaVerne Moore challenged Bing Crosby to a sizeable wager on a round of golf. Moore was certainly a good player, but Crosby must have felt confident he would win given that a condition of the bet was that LaVerne wasn't going to use golf clubs, but simply a rake, a hoe and a baseball bat. Bing sadly still lost the game. Exactly how LaVerne played isn't recorded, but it's likely he used the baseball bat as a driver, the rake as a putter, and the hoe probably just offered moral support.

THE EUROPEAN ROULETTE WHEEL HAS ONE GREEN SLOT NUMBERED 0. THE HOUSE ADVANTAGE ON THIS WHEEL IS 2.7%

Matri-money

A woman who struck lucky in the California lottery took home $1.3 million, but was then stripped of her winnings by a court. The reason? She booted out her husband and divorced him just after the windfall, without telling him about it. This was considered fraud and she had to give him not half but the entire amount. All in all, on her part it was definitely a bananas split.

Huck Up

A professional poker player once bet a fellow pro $5,000 that he could beat him in a 50-yard dash hopping on one foot (with the other guy running normally). The story goes that the hopper watched his colleague run a warm-up sprint, realized he didn't have a chance and just paid over the cash without even trying. A hop-less effort if ever there was one.

Football Flutter

In the 2002 World Cup, England's prospects looked quite healthy, what with the team being in the quarter-finals of the competition. Unfortunately they faced the might of Brazil, but that didn't stop one zealous England fan betting £100,000 on his team to win the trophy. Sadly England lost (2-1, thanks to Ronaldinho's "expertly guided" free kick) and so did the punter. Come on, betting on England to win the World Cup? A new dictionary definition of optimism indeed.

THE AMERICAN ROULETTE WHEEL HAS TWO GREEN SLOTS (0 AND 00). THIS GIVES THE HOUSE AN ADVANTAGE OF 5.3%. PLAY ROULETTE IN EUROPE!

Don't Lose It

The Chopard Blue Diamond Ring, valued at $16.26 million, is the most expensive ring in the world. Any girl would find it hard to say no to a proposal based around that. Even one of marriage. But if the engagement is going to be that expensive just imagine how much the divorce would cost.

What a Sack

An Aussie investment advisor was jailed in January 2009 for running a scheme which promised high returns to investors, but which actually involved spending their money – AUD$1.3 million dollars of it. His clients were obviously caught financially half-asleep, but at least it wasn't a whopping pokie loss this time.

Sister Act

For 40 years two American sisters saved almost every penny they ever earned. By 1991 they had managed to amass a $1.2 million fortune between them which they intended to use to purchase a retirement home and a dream holiday in Italy. In a push for greater returns they decided to move their investment to a brokerage firm which promised them huge profits. What they got were huge losses. Every risky investment failed and the interest rates changed seemingly just to spite them. Eventually they lost almost all of their savings. Still, at least they had each other to rely on afterwards. Or someone to blame anyway.

A SURVEY ESTIMATED THAT A THIRD OF ALL FOOD PURCHASED IN THE UK ENDS UP IN THE BIN

Market Forces

An American stock-market trader managed to ruin himself financially in 2008 by holding a trade open over the course of a long weekend. While he was away from his desk, the market went into a shock nose-dive, plummeting for three days straight. Discovering his massive three-day loss, he sold up swiftly, only to watch in horror as the market then rebounded the following morning.

Party Popper

In 1957, a financier threw a special party, inviting 140 people, plus guests, to quaff the finest champagne and dine on some of the best, most exotic food money could buy. Just an everyday display of moneyed excess you'd think. Except the party was to celebrate his becoming bankrupt, and everyone on the guest list was an unpaid creditor. His plan wasn't entirely suicidal – he wanted to assure them that he still had some money and would pay them all back as soon as possible. Unfortunately he couldn't afford to pay the caterers so while the champagne was still fizzy, the rest of the party fell very flat.

Baccarat Disaster

A Japanese property developer reportedly lost $10 million at baccarat in a week at the Trump Plaza casino. It was certainly one short step from real-estate to a real state.

Pig Sick

Years of hard graft in Libya gave a Philippine couple just enough money to start a pig farm. The company they bought the set up from didn't bother providing feed on time however, so the piglets ended up dying or becoming wasted. The couple had to abandon the farm, taking nothing but debts with them. It's a shame they didn't start a poultry farm instead, because then they'd only have been dealing with chicken feed.

Brown Smacker

A bank employee cost her boss £10,000 when she took up his bet. He said none of the staff would dare go up to Gordon Brown and kiss him at a charity function they were attending. She did just that, and he was obliged to donate the ten grand to a good cause. Next time perhaps the boss will up the betting stakes, and she'll be able to strike a real blow for charity.

A Short Cut

The *Sunday Times* Rich List estimated that celebrity hairdresser John Frieda's personal wealth was cut by about £40 million in 2009. Seeing as that's around a quarter of his finances, it's a bit more than just a trim. He could probably disguise the loss by adding layers and using some volume-enhancing shampoo.

WITH FIVE CARDS DEALT IN POKER, THE PROBABILITY OF GETTING FOUR OF A KIND IS 1 IN 4,000

Vegas Victim

An enigmatic Chinese high-roller is a frequent visitor to the lights and betting tables of Las Vegas. Over the last few years, he has apparently lost more than $125 million. Did I say enigmatic? I meant idiotic.

Pump Up The Price

A UK petrol station owner decided to make the most of 2000's fuel crisis by doubling his prices. He made money briefly but then his supplier forced him to remove their logo from his forecourt, and customers deserted him. He went bust as a result shortly afterwards. His own fault for being such a greedy fuel.

Milking A Good Idea

Hugh McIntosh took a bold business gamble in the 1930s and opened a string of bars selling milkshakes to the London masses. These proved extremely popular and he made a lot of money at first but then other people started to get in on the act (unlike the kid in the famous white chocolate adverts, the Milk Bars weren't only on him). His milk business turned sour and he was forced to call in the liquidators having lost everything (you'd have thought he'd have creamed a bit off the top at least).

IN THE U.S. OVER 70 MILLION DECKS OF PLAYING CARDS ARE SOLD EACH YEAR

Boiler Blues

In February 2009, a Cornish man got taken in by a so-called boiler room scam, stumping up £6,000 for a bunch of totally worthless shares. Operating usually from abroad (and not out of an airing cupboard as you might expect), the name derives from the effective high pressure sales techniques these scammers have cultivated. Bring back double-glazing cold-calls, all is forgiven.

Dodgy Drive

Driveway paving scams are quite common in America, whereby workmen arrive at your house having apparently just completed a job elsewhere. The say they have just enough asphalt left over to do your drive, and offer a cheap price. In reality, they merely lay down a very thin top layer of asphalt and vamoose. It soon cracks up and the number on their business card turns out to be a false one. One old lady in the state of Alabama was intimidated into paying almost $100,000 for a driveway she didn't want. A crazy amount for paving. Where did she get that kind of money from anyway? Must have had a hell of a lot of biscuit tins under her bed.

Drink from the Drink

Ten bottles of 1907 vintage Heidsieck Champagne were salvaged from the seabed in 2008 and sold at the Ritz-Carlton in Moscow for $275,000 a pop. Spend your money on that and you really would be pissing it away, although at least that would be returning it to the sea.

Swede Slump

Ingvar Kamprad might not be a name you're familiar with, but he's a very wealthy man. The richest in Europe, in fact. According to a 2009 Forbes report, tough times of late have left him down an estimated $9 billion. Ingvar founded Ikea, a name you probably are familiar with, and coincidentally the company has lost 9 billion too. Not dollars, that's the number of screws and Allen keys that have gone missing from coffee table kits down through the years, according to the bureau of silly and completely made up facts.

Gemmy Bear

German teddy makers Steiff produced a special bear to celebrate their 125th anniversary. A luxury model with a mouth made of gold, and sapphires and diamonds inset on the eyes (a bling bear, if you will). Someone paid $193,000 for one of these teddies, apparently. And if that's not a bear-faced waste of money, I don't know what is.

Fuller Shit

In the nineteenth century, "Mad Jack" Fuller was visiting London when he bet a friend a large sum of money that the church spire of Dallington village was visible from his house. When he got home, he realized it wasn't due to a hill being in the way. So he organised labourers to quickly build a replica of the spire on a nearby ridge where it could be seen. When his friend arrived the next day he couldn't deny that he could see the spire of Dallington church. And apparently agreed to pay up, even though Jack had clearly conned him. Con-spired against him, even.

Cash For Questions

In 1998, former Conservative MP Neil Hamilton took Harrods owner Mohamed Al-Fayed to court for libel after being accused of accepting money to ask questions on his behalf in the House of Commons. He lost the case, appealed, lost again and was made bankrupt. To make back the £3 million it was reported he owed, Hamilton, along with his wife Christine, turned to showbiz, appearing on numerous TV programmes including *Mastermind*. He probably found it odd to be answering questions for money, rather than asking them.

Stamps a Million

The most valuable stamp in the world is the Swedish "Treskilling Yellow" which was printed in the wrong colour. It's believed to be a one-off, although its original owner didn't realize that, and sold it in the late nineteenth century for just 7 Kronor. A few years later it fetched 4,000 Guilder, which must have made the original seller green (or indeed yellow) with envy. Even more so when you consider that in 1996, a century later, it was sold for around $2 million. At that price, it should come with its own butler to lick it for you (the stamp that is).

GT-Oh Crap

The Ferrari 250 GTO is an expensive classic car. Really expensive. In 2008, it's rumoured that an anonymous English car enthusiast paid $28 million for one. And the owner of one of these ridiculously valuable motors not only had the brass balls to actually drive it, but on a race track, too. And he (or she, let's not be sexist) piled it into the back of another car. Them's the brakes, and it's a shame the driver couldn't find them. That way they might have avoided what must be the costliest single car accident in automotive history.

Expensive Trip

A man visiting a museum in Cambridge tripped over his shoelace and fell down the stairs, into a collection of 300-year-old Chinese vases. Valued at £100,000, the Qing Dynasty vases were smashed on the floor. Turning them into Fling Dynasty vases. Possibly.

Land Larks #1

In 1879, Ramon Vigil sold over 30,000 acres of land in New Mexico for $4,000 to Padre Thomas Aquinas Hayes. Just five years later, after selling and buying it back once in a clever scheme to jack up the asking price, Hayes sold it again for a cool $100,000. Ramon must have been gutted. The Padre also apparently left the new owners lumbered with a couple of lawsuits, which was very nice of him. Love thy neighbour and do unto others... Unless thy can shaft him in a land package deal in which case fill thy boots.

Sinking Feeling

One of the greatest maritime disasters was that of the *Titanic* in 1912. The "unsinkable" ship hit an iceberg and sank, with over 1,500 people losing their lives. The giant vessel cost $7.5 million to build, which would be a lot more in today's money, although probably still not quite as much as the $200 million film. $7.5 million would barely get you a Di Caprio butt cheek these days.

IN POKER IF YOU'RE "UNDER THE GUN" IT MEANS YOU'RE FIRST TO PLAY, THE MOST UNDESIRABLE POSITION TO BE IN

Poker Fleece

Between 2005 and 2007, a popular online poker website was allegedly hit by cheaters who exploited code to look at their opponent's cards. How things have come on since marked decks. The security holes have now been resolved apparently, although a claim for $75 million was filed against the company.

Family Misfortune #1

A family moving to Arizona thought they had rented their ideal home. They met the couple that owned it, made arrangements to swiftly move in, signed the lease and handed over a $1,500 deposit. The next day they cleaned the house, and the day after that they cheerfully arrived with their belongings to move in. Only to find the owner at home – the real owner, that is, who didn't have a clue what they were babbling on about when they said they were the tenants. Leaving them high and dry and needing to find another rental. The motto of the story: Act in haste, re-rent at leisure.

Dog 'Nabbit

A couple received an email from Nigeria (hmm, any alarm bells ringing with anyone?) asking if they would look after some African missionary's dog, which needed re-homing. They happily sent $350 off to cover shipping the animal, but – gasp, horror – the dog never arrived. Unsurprisingly, they had been shafted, and in the missionary position too.

Kingly Wager

Princess Feodora of Denmark married Prince Christian of Schaumburg-Lippe (a small state in Germany) in 1937. Feodora's uncle, King Christian, clearly seeing nothing wrong with gambling with the priest on his niece's wedding day, bet the clergyman one Danish crown that the wedding tram would arrive on a particular side of the track. He lost the bet and handed over the money, quipping, "That's the first time I have lost my crown."

Tickets On Himself

Interesting fact: the Chinese lottery is the only one in the world where your lucky numbers can also correspond with your favourite meal. And in 2005 a Chinese ticket vendor was licking his lips and preparing himself up for a slap-up banquet when he discovered a flaw in the lottery system. He realized he could purchase tickets a few minutes after the draw had been made, filling in the correct numbers to win. Using his friends to cash them he made almost $4 million, but two years later his fraud was uncovered and he had the lot confiscated. He also got handed a life sentence and the realisation that the only lottery he was going to be involved in henceforth was the prison showers.

THE ODDS OF WINNING THE AMERICAN POWERBALL LOTTERY ARE 1 IN 195,249,054

Pearly King

August Rehfelt made a bet on the result of the 1895 Republican County Convention, and lost. His forfeit was to treat the entire crowd to an oyster supper, but in the end the sheer number of people made this rather unrealistic (too expensive, and not enough oysters to go round) so another penalty was devised – Rehfelt would eat 90 oysters himself. He started well, but after 50 or so began to struggle, and when he hit 81 his eyes bulged out and he became violently ill. Dr Sickles was called in (no, seriously) and Rehfelt spent the next few days recuperating and, presumably, shitting out the occasional pearl necklace.

Heavenly Heist

A woman was conned out of $10,000 by a pair of brothers who operated a scam in California. They claimed to have a direct line to God (an option that's seemingly missing on most mobile contracts), and apparently convinced people by performing simple tricks such as turning water into wine (or at least Ribena). The woman in question reportedly paid them the ten grand to rid her daughter of a curse, which to be fair they did, when they walked out the door after being paid.

Car Fool

A English man who advertised his car for sale on the Internet received interest from a Dutch buyer who offered to pay shipping costs on top of the asking price. The deal was accepted and the seller was sent a bankers draft for more than the agreed amount (to cover shipping and expenses) and asked to return any surplus. He cashed the draft in, and being honest, immediately sent back the left-over cash, some £3,500. It was only after the amount had been taken from his account, that his bank informed him that the original draft was a fake. Still, at least he got to keep the car. Not that he wanted it...

Restless Gambler

A patient who took a certain drug for her restless leg syndrome soon discovered that they had an unwanted side effect. They certainly helped her condition, but allegedly led her to develop a compulsive gambling habit whereby she couldn't stop herself from visiting the local casino and risking huge sums of money on the tables. She went from shuffling feet to shuffling cards, and that transition cost her a reported $140,000 in losses. Not much use ridding yourself of restless leg syndrome if you're going to suffer restless wallet syndrome instead.

THE DEAD MAN'S HAND, HELD BY WILD BILL HICKOCK WHEN HE WAS SHOT, IS TWO PAIRS OF BLACK ACES AND BLACK EIGHTS

Fridge Magnet

In the 1986 Superbowl, a bookmaker offered odds of 20 to 1 that William Perry, a man-mountain 300 pound plus defensive tackler that the Chicago Bears occasionally used in the backfield, would score a touchdown. Maybe they felt safe because Bears coach Mike Ditka said they weren't going to use him on offence, but when the team built a commanding lead Ditka put him in. Lo and behold the lumbering behemoth found himself in the endzone with the ball, and the bookmaker lost huge amounts of cash to Bears fans on the odds he'd been given. Perry's nickname was the "Refrigerator", because he was the size of a fridge. Either that or because he spent all his free time with his head in one.

Mirror Mirror On The Wall

Who is the ugliest of them all? That's the question Lord Chesterfield asked in the seventeenth century, as there was a Swiss opera impresario by the name of John Heidegger who was reputed to be the ugliest man in the country. (He was so ugly, when he was born the doctor thought the afterbirth had come out first). But Chesterfield said he'd seen uglier and promptly entered into a bet of some 50 guineas that he could find someone more repulsive.

The story goes that he was confident when he found a particularly hideous crone, but Heidegger pinched her hat and donned it, the sight of which caused her to faint. Chesterfield lost his cash, but could at least wear headgear without causing a horse and carriage accident.

THE FIRST GREYHOUND RACE IN BRITAIN WAS HELD IN MANCHESTER IN 1926

Bingoing Crazy

In 1966, an English woman lost her housekeeping money playing bingo. She decided to get it back by breaking into a casino and jemmying some cash out of the one-arm bandits. The mother of five was caught, fined £5 and ordered to stay away from bingo halls (but not, oddly, from casinos with slot machines). She was more than happy to comply, stating "I'll never go to the bingo again." She then shouted "88!" loudly, causing two large passing women to turn and stare.

Old Kent Woes

A couple from England both lost their jobs in 2009, and couldn't keep up the payments on their mortgage. Luckily, they had a place to move out to when they were evicted from their home. Unluckily, that place was a rented lock-up garage. Wonder what council tax band that is?

Ross Loss

Carphone Warehouse co-founder David Ross had a rough time of it after real-estate deals he got involved in went bad. In 2008 his net worth reportedly declined from an estimated $1.4 billion to just $150 million, and he probably had to change his ringtone from "Who wants to be a billionaire..."

GREYHOUND RACING DOESN'T INVOLVE A TINY JOCKEY SITTING ON THE BACK OF THE DOG AND TRYING TO WHIPPET

Asylum Seeker

In 1890, Alexander Miller, an official of the State Asylum in Denver Colorado, was fleeced out of £100 while holidaying in England. He reported his having been conned out of the money to the United States Consul in London, but was unable to state how or where he had actually been robbed. Which suggests he might have been less of an official of the State Asylum and more of a guest...

Call Me

An English clerk stole £8,000 from the company he worked for to pay off the bills he'd racked up calling premium rate chat lines. Wonder if he told all the sexy ladies about his adventures afterwards?

Go Diego Go

Diego.com sold for $58,830 in 2009. Presumably it reached that figure as the result a fierce battle between several people called Diego. Or a hefty bid from a drive-through undertakers.

THE SUICIDE RATE OF PATHOLOGICAL GAMBLERS IS 20 TIMES HIGHER THAN FOR NON-GAMBLERS

Buy-to-Lose

In 2009, five buy-to-let scammers pleaded guilty to defrauding property investors out of approximately £80 million. The Serious Fraud Office said they operated a ponzi-style scheme, returning investors' money back to them parading as rental profits, and using funds to pay themselves extravagant salaries. Mind you, they made a few crackers investments of their own, like spending an alleged half a million pounds on a Christmas works-do.

Land Boom

In 1920s America, the state of Florida started to become more popular, with increasing numbers of people moving there due to its warm climate. As sales began to grow faster than the number of homes being built, demand and prices rose steeply. And this attracted investors who smelt profits, which further stoked demand – a classic real-estate bubble. Stories abound of properties being sold multiple times in one day. But like all bubbles it eventually burst in 1925, when people began to realize prices had got absurdly high, and investors who had bought in with the intention of "flipping" (immediately selling on) for a quick profit couldn't sell. Prices nose-dived, worsened by hurricane strikes and then the Great Depression, leaving countless Florida investors bereft of small fortunes.

Racist Forfeits

In 1888, lawyer E.M. Friend made a bet with fellow lawyer F.B. House that President Grover Cleveland would again win the election and be returned to office. When he lost, Mr Friend cheerfully accepted his punishment which was to parade along New York's Broadway in the "outfit of a plantation darky." Had Mr House lost, he would have followed the same route, dressed as a "Chinese laundryman." E.M. Friend should have known better than to make the wager of course, because everyone knows "the House always wins."

Dusty Denims

In 2005, an anonymous Japanese collector bought a pair of 115 year old Levi's jeans in an eBay auction. Forget your designer jeans, these old pants held together by sweat, grime and Lord knows what else became the most expensive jeans in the world, according to the *Guinness Book of Records* at the time. The buyer spent a trouser-pocket-popping $60,000 on them. Let's just hope they fitted okay – if they were too roomy around the middle they'd have been a big waist of money. Or if the jeans were too long in the leg that would be almost as bad. Then they'd be turn-ups Japanese, yes they'd be turn-ups Japanese, I really think so.

Skytrain Crash

In 1977, Freddie Laker launched Skytrain, his no-frills transatlantic budget airline. Like all trains in Britain, it ran a little late – taking six and a half years longer than anticipated to get off the ground (the airline, not the first plane). Flights initially ran between London and New York although additional destinations were later added. Despite its success, Laker Airways was a wholly private airline and the economic recession of the early 1980s proved to be too much turbulence for it to weather. The company went bankrupt in 1982 with debts of £270 million.

Michigan Millionaire #1

In 1977, a man won $1 million in the Michigan lottery with a 50-cent ticket. He moved to California and used the money to open stores specialising in pool tables, but just a few years later business turned bad and he ended up filing for bankruptcy. There's a kind of gambling poetry here – what he won on the lottery, he lost on the pools.

Call 911

A man who bought a $50,000 Porsche 911 on eBay got quite a shock when he wired the money across. The whole thing was a con and he never heard from the seller again. And you thought nobody fell for those penis extension scams any more.

Red Widow

A millionaire widow who thought she had over $7 million invested in Bernard Madoff's pyramid scam lost the lot. One of the New York financier's many victims (see the Top Ten Reasons Not To Trust the Money Men), she is now working doing cleaning and laundry. Well and truly hung out to dry.

Missing Millionaire

A not-so-lucky American scooped a $3.1 million lottery prize in 1989. Inside two years he'd apparently blown the lot on a divorce and cocaine. Thus proving the lottery's not all it's cracked up to be.

Rigged Match

In 1973, former male Wimbledon champion Bobby Riggs took on reigning women's champion Billie Jean King in a "Battle of the Sexes" tennis match. An estimated worldwide TV audience of 40 million saw King thrash Riggs in straight sets and take home the £80,000 prize. She had a slight advantage though. Riggs last won Wimbledon in 1939 and at 55 he was a little out of shape, partially deaf, didn't have the greatest eyesight and his health routine involved swallowing 400 vitamins a day (surprised the rattling didn't put Billie Jean off her game). Still he had every right to be confident, as earlier in the year he'd beaten the world number one ladies player, Margaret Court.

Gambled His Career Away

In 1933, after 27 years working for the Crown Agents for the Colonies, Frederick Stokoe had a decent job and a reasonable salary. He also had a serious gambling habit and owed £800 (nearly two years' worth of wages). Gambling to get it back hadn't worked, so he decided to steal it from his employer instead. He was caught, tried and found guilty of theft and fraud. His defence council observed somewhat unhelpfully afterwards, "he'll lose a good pension."

Bug Apple

We're used to slick Apple products these days, but back in 1980 when the company launched the Apple III computer things were different. Not only was it expensive at $4,000 (for the basic model, $8,000 for the top end), it was a design nightmare, suffering from numerous software, hardware and overheating problems. To the extent that the first 14,000 computers sold had to be replaced by Apple, free of charge. In total only around 65,000 were shifted in the four years it was on the market, and it's said Apple lost around $60 million on the project.

Perhaps the best known story about the Apple III is a supposed technical advisory from the company which dealt with the problem of the computer's chips coming loose in their sockets. The official solution? Pick up the machine and drop it on the desk to reseat them. Maybe better advice would have been to do that, but while standing over a bin instead.

IN THE UK, PRIZE DRAW SCAMS ARE THOUGHT TO HOODWINK 500,000 VICTIMS OUT OF SOME £320 MILLION EVERY YEAR

Heist The Aged

A Welsh financial advisor cheated eight elderly clients out of a whopping £163,000. He got his comeuppance however, when he was eventually caught and sentenced to two years in jail. He was also ordered to pay over more than £100,000 in compensation or have his sentence increased by an additional three years. Wonder who he went to for advice on that particular financial problem?

Give It Away Now #1

An American woman landed $18 million in a lottery win in 1993. She then donated a lot of money to a number of political and local community causes. All very commendable, but perhaps she gave just a little bit too much away seeing as she reportedly went bankrupt after eight years.

Rugger Bugger

A high-stakes gambler placed a colossal NZD$5.8 million wager on the All Blacks winning the 2007 Rugby World Cup. He was kept anonymous by the betting agency he used, but there's a good chance he was a Kiwi. Of course, New Zealand were knocked out in the quarter-finals and South Africa won the tournament. Leaving his bank account probably not all in the black.

Sink Us Victorious

HMS *Victory*, the predecessor to Lord Nelson's Victory, sank during a fierce storm in 1744. More than a thousand sailors drowned and its cargo of four tons of gold, worth around £400,000 then (and £700 million now) went to the bottom of the sea. The ship was commanded by 74-year-old Admiral Sir John Balchin, who'd come out of retirement especially for one final voyage (prophetically as it turned out). A true case of grasping defeat from the jaws of Victory.

2005: A Space Oddity

In 2006, a man from America bought an egg for $10,000. Was it a gold one, and did it come with the goose that laid it? No. It was green, and worse still, it was an item in an online computer game, with no known function or point. In 2005 the same player also bought a virtual space station in the game for a mind blowing $100,000. In fairness, apparently he's made a profit from this move, as other players pay to use it. But even so, that's a ridiculous sum for what's essentially some pixels on a monitor screen. I just hope he had a survey done ("1,000 apartment luxury space resort with ship docking facilities... Some heat shield tiles need re-pointing... No evidence of space damp... May blink out of existence if server goes down.") If anyone's interested I've got a spare recycle bin icon on my desktop, one previous owner, only 4,522 empties on the clock. Yours for just £50.

Eubank-rupt

Retired middleweight champion Chris Eubank is said to have earned a £35 million fortune during his career. However, the eccentric ex-boxer went bankrupt in 2005, owing a monocle-popping £1.3 million in taxes. At least he's still "Lord of the Manor" of Brighton, which apparently gives him rights to 4,000 herring a year. A fishy title if ever there was one.

General Malfunction

General Motors did not perform well over 2008 with the fall in demand for new cars. GM faced losses of $21 billion on its operations over the year, according to Fortune magazine, and in June 2009 filed for bankruptcy, making it the biggest industrial failure in U.S. corporate history. The company's dicey performance could be summed up in two words: GM craps.

Wheel Shame

A contestant made a costly slip on the *Wheel of Fortune* show in the U.S. in 2007. She had the entire puzzle on the board minus one letter, and stood to win $33,000 and a $6,000 bonus holiday. She knew the missing letter, and basically all she had to do was read out the answer. A shame, then, that on the very last word she said "beaches" instead of "beach." The rules are if you don't say the phrase exactly, the answer is deemed wrong. She lost the cash, not being quick thinking enough to claim she had a sporadic lisp that had just flared up.

THE MILLENNIUM DOME IN LONDON COST £750 MILLION. A GMTV SURVEY REVEALED 3/4 OF THE UK POPULATION THOUGHT IT WAS A WASTE OF MONEY

Trike a Light

In January 1985, the first launch from Sinclair Vehicles was rolled out. It would have been driven out, but frankly they couldn't find anyone thick-skinned and stupid enough to clamber into the three-wheeled embarrassment that was the C5. The vehicular brainchild of Sir Clive Sinclair was, essentially, a battery assisted tricycle.

With its very low profile, not only did it make you look an arse, but you were also potentially invisible to other motorists. It cost in the region of £12 million to develop, but between its comical appearance and safety concerns only 17,000 C5s were sold. Still, if you were one of those few C5 drivers, the vehicle did make you feel lucky to be alive. Not because you owned one, but because you'd arrived at your destination without being splattered all over the underside of a truck.

Riddle of the Sphinx

Maurice Roth was a serious gambler prepared to wager large sums of money on just about anything. He had a lucky mascot in the shape of a brass sphinx (with a naked woman figure hidden inside) that he believed controlled his good fortune. In 1938, after a run of bad luck, he drowned himself and was found with the sphinx still in his pocket. He might have been better off just chucking that in the water.

Last Resort

Bugsy Siegel was a gangster (with a name like that, he had to be), though in later life he went into real-estate and developed a Las Vegas hotel and casino, the Flamingo. The mob invested in the project, but things went badly, and by 1946 the budget had overrun severely at $6 million. Which included lavish extras such as a $1 million sewage system for the hotel – a literal waste of money. Even when the resort opened, it still wasn't quite finished. Siegel, however, was, as the money coming in wasn't sufficient to redeem for his cock-ups. Bugsy flung his last flamingo when he was shot in the eye (and not with ice cream like in the film).

Clowning Around

Henry Hooper was a clown. The circus performer who had once sung for Queen Victoria received a sizeable inheritance from his mother but drank much of it away and lost the rest when his brother declared bankruptcy while still owing him a chunk of cash. He eventually ran out of money and hanged himself behind a kitchen door – reports don't mention whether or not he was wearing his clown outfit at the time.

South Seasick

One of the most disastrous financial bubbles in British history began in 1711 with the foundation of the South Sea Company. This was a group of merchants who secured a monopoly on trade with South America in 1720, and with visions of the imagined piles of gold they were going to hoodwink from the natives, investors piled in with wads of cash. Such was the demand the company's stock rocketed tenfold, and Brits who had plenty of disposable income at the time were soon all looking to invest in the market. Not only in the SSC, but a raft of ridiculous companies that sprang up to take advantage of the suckers.

One new firm planned to produce a gun that fired square cannon balls, and another was set up to explore the profitable market of hair trading. But best of all was a business which promised to "Carry out an undertaking of great advantage, but nobody is to know what it is." Apparently £2,000 was sunk into this by the British public, unbelievably. Needless to say this unfettered optimistic investment imploded when the badly run South Sea Company came unstuck, and the cries of "buy" turned to "sell" in September of 1720. Much of a whole generation had their savings wiped out. Hair trading today, gone tomorrow...

Shitty Performance

In 2008, banking behemoth Citigroup reported a net loss of nearly $19 billion, hit hard by the subprime mortgages debacle. Which I think is something to do with giving mortgages to substandard cows. Cows don't have money, you say? Hogwash. What do you think they do with the spare change from all the cow tipping that goes on.

Unlicensed to Bill

In 2007 an international firm that wasn't named was slapped with an – at the time – record $3.5 million fine for having "significant shortfalls in software licenses." The silly billies had obviously forgotten to key in their serial numbers and lost their discs, very careless. I wonder if it was a shipbuilding business with a lot of one-legged employees and parrot fanciers on board?

Chicken and Bacon Sandwich

Farmer P.B. Lespenasse bet on the outcome of the 1885 presidential election and lost. Rather than pay up the money he owed he made use of a clause in the wager which allowed him to instead walk from New York to Washington, with a pig under one arm, and a rooster under the other. He was able to defray his expenses along the way by selling photos of his cock. And of the pig as well.

Bombers Away

In 2008, a B-2 stealth bomber, the *Spirit of Kansas*, crashed just after take-off from an airbase in Guam. Investigators blamed lashing rain which had evidently entered the plane's sensor system and caused on-board computers to malfunction and stall the B-2. Both pilots survived but the *Spirit of Kansas* was a write-off, and a bloody expensive one at that. The B-2 cost $1.4 billion, making this the most expensive aviation accident ever. And all because of a touch of electrical pain, caused by rain, which fell mainly on the plane.

Beeb Blooper #1

In 2008, the BBC lost £400,000 courtesy of Ofcom, the largest fine they have ever demanded of the corporation. It was over competition phone line shenanigans, whereby staff on a number of different shows were accused of making up fake winners, posing as contestants themselves, and generally not behaving as Auntie Beeb should (unless she's pissed up three sheets to the wind on gin). Still, at least one of the programmes was Comic Relief, so the phoning public were being conned in a good cause.

CYBERCRIME AND ONLINE THEFT COSTS IN THE ORDER OF $1 TRILLION A YEAR

Help Yourself

We all take the odd little thing home from work, don't we?
You know, some A4 paper perhaps, a nice black pen, maybe a
stapler, and not forgetting the odd wad of $10,000 cash. Which
is what one U.S. bank teller helped herself to on multiple
occasions over several years. She now faces embezzlement
charges in excess of $1 million. And I bet they asked for the
stapler back, too.

Bar All

An American bartender caused a tavern owner fiscal woe
when she decided to serve drinks in the nude. The proprietor
was fined $500 and had their liquor license suspended for
a month, which must have cost a hefty amount in takings.
Although I suppose that rather depends on whether or not
she was an ugly moose whose strip had already scared all the
patrons off.

Waste of Eden

The oldest real-estate blunder was surely when a large
paradise garden was swapped for a piece of fruit. Yes, when
Adam and Eve gave up the Garden of Eden for the sake of an
apple. It wasn't just the apple that stuck in Adam's throat, I'm
sure this deal did, too.

Goldie Looking Pain

In 1886, the South African gold rush was on. Gold prospector Sors Hariezon staked a claim to some land near what would later become Johannesburg. Before long he sold it off for a mere $20. Since then, the mines in that area have produced a colossal amount of gold – over 100,000 tons of the stuff. Let's hope he was a better philosopher than he was prospector.

Forty Big Ones

According to the Wisconsin Lottery, over a period of 11 years some $40 million worth of prizes have remained unclaimed. That's a lotta lotta lost lotto loot.

Who Shot PCjr?

In 1984 IBM unveiled the PCjr, a home computer they expected to be a huge success. However, it turned out to be more floppy than a 5.25 inch disk. The project was wound up just one short year later, after sales suffered badly due to a number of problems: It was expensive, had a rubbish keyboard, non-standard expansion ports, and was incompatible with many PC programs. Still, it did make amazing leaps in home computer security with a remarkable yet extremely simple anti-theft system. Namely it was so crap no bugger would bother stealing it.

Memphis Blues

Sam Phillips was a record producer who owned a small recording studio in Memphis. When his business ran into some financial difficulties in 1955, he sold the contract of one of his artists to RCA records for $35,000. And the name of that singer? Elvis Presley. Yes... Oh dear doesn't quite cover it. When Elvis left the building, he took with him future sales in excess of a billion records.

Mome-a-Mia

The 2009 Grand National was won by 100-to-1 outsider Mon Mome, the first French-bred winner in a century. The last one was Lutteur III, which scooped the win in 1909. As there wasn't a whole lot of money placed on the horse, this was great news for most bookies, apart from one poor betting shop in the same area as the nag's stables. Some 700 hopeful locals chanced their arms on Mon Mome, whose name roughly translates as "my child." And at 100 to 1, that must have been a hell of a child support payment the unfortunate bookmaker had to cough up.

Krypton-Rights

When Joe Shuster and Jerry Siegel had their first Superman story published in 1938, they reportedly received $130 for the comic strip. But that sum also included the copyright to the character, which was worth, well, a bit more than that eventually, given all the films and spin-offs. Not to mention the merchandising which flew off the shelves (well not literally, it wasn't quite that authentic).

Amster-Damn Crazy

In the seventeenth century tulips were imported into Holland from Turkey. The novelty of the pretty flower gave rise to a high level of demand amongst the affluent Dutch, but tulips were still rare, so the price rose and people began to speculate on this flower "market." This further drove demand to astonishing levels where a single bulb could fetch up to $5,000 in today's money. They were valued by weight, like gold, and tulip traders made an absolute mint.

Owners wouldn't even plant their bulbs, as they were so valuable they were generally put in display cases. Then in 1637 the inevitable happened – tulip deals started to fall through, and in a blinding moment of clarity people began to realize that tulips were flowers and actually worth f**k all. Panic selling ensued and the bottom fell out of the precious petals market in a big way. Lots of aristocrats lost huge amounts of cash and were left with some very silly looking flower bulbs in toughened glass cases.

FROM 1990 TO 2007, THE AVERAGE AMERICAN'S CREDIT CARD DEBT HAS MORE THAN TRIPLED

Sex Pest

A millionaire who lost his wealth and his company blamed the drugs he was taking for a non-malignant tumour. He claimed the medication gave him a raging and uncontrollable sexual appetite that caused him to spend all of his money on prostitutes, champagne and karaoke. At least he only partially wasted it.

Neigh Way

In the eighteenth century a plucky Brit bet a visiting German a large (undisclosed) sum of money that he couldn't ride his horse backwards all the way from London to Edinburgh. Unfortunately for him, the German did somehow. If that horse was still around today, it would be very old. And working as a Michael Jackson tribute act (what with those crazy moonwalking skills).

Just Not Ticket

A Connecticut lottery player who died of a heart attack had a winning ticket in his pocket for $10 million. Which was very unfortunate for him, although not so much for his wife who found it ("every cloud…" and all that). I would imagine he had a bloody good no-expense spared funeral, though. And possibly a silver lined coffin.

THE GAME OF KENO ORIGINATED IN CHINA, AROUND 200 BC

A Committed Gambler

Sam Greenberg lost all of his money gambling unsuccessfully on the horses. In the three months after he placed his first bet in 1906, he fell so far behind on the rent, his family got evicted. Determined to make things right, but ultimately making them worse, he quit his job to focus on gambling. His wife, Rebecca, at her wits' end, managed to get Sam committed to an asylum on New York's Blackwell's Island (now Roosevelt Island) in an attempt to get him cured. The equivalent of going into rehab today. Shortly afterwards she attempted to take her own life, but failed. She tried again and succeeded this time – proving herself to be much more adept at suicide than Sam was at picking a winner.

20-20 Vision

An Arizona man was an avid gambler who used to drive across to Nevada to place large bets on American football. The story goes that one week he couldn't be bothered to make the hour long trip, so he entered a newspaper contest instead. He had to pick 20 winning teams, and he correctly guessed every single result! The odds of this are over a million to one, but the paper only ran the game for fun with a token few bucks prize. Placing his normal sized multiple thousand dollar bets at such odds, the winnings would have been more astronomical than the Hubble telescope. A definite case of being unlucky in luck.

IT'S THOUGHT THAT AROUND 65 MILLION PEOPLE PLAY POKER IN THE UNITED STATES

News Cast Off

Newsreader Ed Mitchell, who reportedly once earned £100,000 a year, ran up debts of £250,000 through drinking, gambling and easy credit and ended up living rough on a seafront bench after being declared bankrupt. A pretty unfortunate situation to find himself in, especially given his speciality was finance.

Doh Deal

The *Deal or No Deal* gameshow offers contestants a chance to open 22 boxes in the hope that one of them contains £250,000. There are varying amounts in the others, all the way down the scale to 1p. There have been plenty of terribly unlucky games, and in the UK there are 20 plus members of the 1p club, the folks who have walked away with the lowest prize. Impressively, some contestants have achieved even less than that. By taking on a "banker's gamble" and losing, they actually managed to go home with a big fat zero (as, arguably, did their partners).

But the biggest loser in real terms left with more money than that: he scooped £1. The problem was he had £100,000 in his box and swapped it away in the final round for the £1. Gutted. The U.S. version of the show is played for even more money, and therefore boasts even bigger losers. One chap was left with the $1 million box and the $1 box, and was offered $600,000. A damn good offer which he turned down, to walk away with one buck. Indeed you could call that one big buck up.

Stamped On

In 1875, a young Washington man encountered an old tourist and agreed to show him round the city. They struck up a friendship, and after they'd parted, the old chap fell ill. Realising he was dying, he decided to write to the young man and leave him everything. Unfortunately, he used a torn stamp and the post office refused to deliver the envelope. By the time the recipient got the note, the old man had died, and pissed off at not having heard a word back, had given his fortune to an old lady instead.

From Russia with Loot

Tsar Alexander II made a considerable monetary blunder in 1867 when he flogged Alaska, which was then owned by Russia, to the U.S. To be fair to Alexander, he sold it because he feared the Americans were going to steam in and take it by force anyway, but it was the price tag he got badly wrong. The U.S. paid just $7.2 million for the place, which was a relative pittance in terms of the Russian state coffers even at the time.

Mind you, many Americans thought the deal wasn't all that great for them either. The New York press described the land as offering "nothing of value but fur-bearing animals" (which seems a bit harsh on the native Alaskan population). Anyway, as we all know there's nothing of value at all in Alaska. Nothing. Except, of course, its vast reserves of oil. And gold. Alaska's resources are now valued in the region of $100 billion.

Yah-Boo-Sucks

In February 2008, Microsoft stumped up a takeover offer of some $44 billion for web wizards Yahoo. CEO Jerry Yang turned down the $31 per share offer, and Microsoft withdrew the proposal in May. With the increasing popularity of Google, the company saw its net worth diminish to more like half of this amount before Yang vacated the CEO job. A near $20 billion dent that shareholders probably didn't say "Yahoo!" about.

Major Idiot

In 1850, Major William Hall met a man called "Plin" White who claimed to be buying up gold from the Californian mines. Explaining that a lot of capital was needed for such an enterprise he persuaded the Major to lend him $50,000 as collateral for loans, and then just spent it. The Major tried to sue him to get it back, but failed. Thirty years later White came to visit the Major again, said he was sorry, and after chatting for a while asked to borrow $1,300 to pay off a loan. The major agreed but only after being given two envelopes which he was told contained $6,000 worth of securities. Unsurprisingly, they didn't.

24-Hour Party Pooper

Mark Berry, or Bez as he's more commonly known, was the freaky dancing, maracas wielding mascot in seminal 1990s band Happy Mondays. His role in the group, and later Black Grape, clearly didn't require much talent, and presumably didn't pay too well either because Bez has managed to dance his way into bankruptcy twice. Once in 2005, which he was able to get out of thanks to the £50,000 he earned as the winner of that year's *Celebrity Big Brother*, and again in 2008. Bez is the legend who put the mad in the Madchester scene. Just as well the band didn't come from Dorset or he could well have been putting the dork into Dorchester.

Bottomley's Down

English Member of Parliament, Horatio Bottomley, was a typical swindling cad of the early twentieth century. In 1914 he purchased all the horses running in a particular race, and bribed the jockeys to finish in a specific order. Naturally, he then laid down some hefty bets. It was a masterfully arranged scheme, until nature intervened. The race course was by the sea, and a heavy mist drifted in, making it impossible for the race judges to determine who had actually come where.

No winner, or indeed any places, could be declared, although a loser most certainly was – poor old Horatio who must have been crying into his rakish top hat. Although not as much as in 1922 when he was charged with fraud after misappropriating shareholder's funds, and he became a different type of MP. A Member of Prison.

A SCOTTISH MAN HAS WAGERED £2 AT 5,000 TO 1 THAT A COMET WILL HIT THE EARTH IN THE YEAR 2116

Fool's Gold

There would be no return to boom and bust, the British Prime Minister famously assured his citizens in the midst of a boom decade which has led to potentially the biggest bust since Lolo Ferrari stumbled onto the set of Eurotrash. And Gordon Brown's handling of the nation's gold reserves was about as adept as his economic prophecy.

Back in 1999 when he was chancellor, Gordon decided to sell off around half of the UK's gold. Despite the fact that, according to newspaper reports, top gold traders warned against this action as the price of the metal generally moves in decade-long cycles and an upturn was likely on the cards.

Not only did Brown sell, but the plans were announced in advance. Thus the market price fell in anticipation, driven down to a 20-year-low as the treasury began to unload around 400 tons of bullion over the next few years. These sort of breathtaking economic negotiation skills haven't been seen since the Inuit finance minister famously inked that deal to buy 400 tons of snow.

And the actual results of the sale? The UK made $3.5 billion. Since then, the price of gold has rocketed, and if sold today could expect to achieve more in the order of $10 billion. It all amounts to a definitely not-so golden Brown moment.

THE TOTAL REVENUE FROM COLORADO CASINOS DROPPED 12% TO $716 MILLION IN 2008

Oh Crumbs

An heiress ran into some serious financial trouble in 1993. According to reports, the woman, heir to a savoury baked product fortune, was left owing a packet. When she was eventually made bankrupt, that probably took the biscuit.

On a Limb

In 2009, Bionic.com sold for $12,000. A tad under the $6 million the man selling it might have been hoping for.

Henry's Hooray

King Henry VIII was fond of the odd flutter, and a cool gambler who never lost his head (though the same can't be said of his wives). Apparently he took part in one rather odd wager in which he lost the bells of St Paul's Cathedral to Sir Miles Partridge. Bet he was pretty brassed off about that. It must have been an interesting game, anyway...

Henry VIII: "I'll raise you a massive bell and a large donger."

Sir Miles: "Are we still playing dice?"

WITH FIVE CARDS DEALT IN POKER, THE PROBABILITY OF GETTING A ROYAL FLUSH IS 1 IN 650,000

Own Goal

It's September 29th 2001 and Tottenham Hotspur are thrashing Manchester United at home. With a half-time score of 3-0, it looks like an easy win for Spurs. That's what one unnamed fan thinks anyway, and he decides to put his money where his mouth is, staking his entire mortgage on Spurs to win. Cue the second half whistle and Man United bang in five past Tottenham with no reply to win the match 5-3. That'll teach him to bet on the Spurs of the moment.

Iridiocy

In 1998, Iridium launched its $5 billion satellite telephone service with heavy financial backing from Motorola. However, inside a year Iridium had fallen into bankruptcy. It failed for a number of reasons – the units were bulky, reportedly unreliable, and of course at the time terrestrial mobile phones had really started to take off. Something that, you would have hoped, Motorola should possibly have been aware of. Perhaps I'll give the CEO of the company a ring now, and maybe they'll go for my innovative new communications device. It involves yoghurt pots (painted silver) and string. Got to be worth a couple of million, surely?

Look Who's Walking

Wall Street banker John Van Schaick made a wager in 1909 that he could walk from his town house to his summer home, a distance of 35 miles. With his friends there to cheer him on (or more precisely to make sure he didn't cheat and cadge a lift), the "portly" Schaick set off at 6am. Nine hours later, having covered 22 miles, his legs became so stiff he could no longer put one foot in front of the other and had to get into a car to be taken the rest of the way. Presumably he could only get walking again once someone had advised him to Schaick a leg.

Roger, Over and Out

Back in the 1980s, a high-flying financial advisor attracted clients including famous authors, singers and actors, and even some athletics stars. Come 1990, however, it all went sour when investigators from FIMBRA descended on his operation and allegedly discovered he'd been fiddling his accounts. It turned out his company was in debt by some £34 million, and had lost a lot of celebrity moolah. He faced serious fraud charges. And ended up with 180 hours community service, somehow. They might well have slapped his wrist and called him a naughty boy, too.

SHAKESPEARE'S "FIRST FOLIO", A COLLECTION OF 36 PLAYS, SOLD FOR AROUND $5 MILLION AT AUCTION IN 2006

Suitcase Man

William Lee Bergstrom from Texas is the famous suitcase gambler. No, he didn't used to bet on whether or not his luggage would be present on the conveyor belt after a long haul flight. Rather, in 1980 Bergstrom arrived at Binions, a Las Vegas casino, with a suitcase filled with $777,000 (nothing suspicious about that) and another empty suitcase. The second was for his winnings, he declared, and stuck all the money on the Don't Pass line in a craps game. He promptly won and doubled his stake, but the story doesn't end there.

He won a few more times after that, but Bergstrom's real ambition was to make a full-on one million dollar bet, and he did so in 1984. Again he played craps, but this time the dice fell badly, and suddenly never mind the suitcases, a matchbox was enough for him to carry his winnings out of the casino in. Three months later, William committed suicide in a hotel, and depending on who you believe, either shot, poisoned himself, or took an overdose. Unlike his famous money bearing luggage, it sounds like it was far from an open and shut case.

Bacca-Rats #2

In just two months in 1997, an Australian casino is alleged to have lost AUD$55 million to big stakes baccarat players. Rumours that the amount of steam coming out of the casino owner's ears contributed greatly to global warming were likely exaggerated.

1,300 COMPANIES WERE PLACED INTO ADMINISTRATION IN THE FIRST QUARTER OF 2009 IN ENGLAND AND WALES

Unlucky for Many

Apparently one ridiculous way to lose a fortune is simply to live in Belfast. According to a survey compiled by Virgin Games which examined a wealth of wagers across the country, it's the unluckiest place to bet in the UK. Which certainly flies in the face of one old saying – perhaps it should be "the suck of the Irish."

Unlucky for One

An English man was dubbed Britain's "unluckiest punter" by the media after he lost out on a near £1 million horse racing jackpot. He had placed a six horse bet, and they all came in first, but the twist was that stewards later disqualified the winner of the final race. With only five winners his payout was just £90. A few weeks later a guy from Manchester who won a similar multiple bet heard his tale of woe, and planned to share some of his own winnings as a goodwill gesture. However, the hapless gambler passed away just before this philanthropic cheque was due to be presented. It really wasn't his year...

Oh, Canada...

A Canadian embezzled over $10 million from the bank that employed him, which he splurged in a wild gambling spree over some 18 months. He was eventually caught and arrested, but did his time and took up a new career as a financial advisor. Or living personification of irony, depending on your viewpoint.

IN CANADA THERE ARE A HIGHER PERCENTAGE OF TEENAGE PATHOLOGICAL GAMBLERS THAN THERE ARE ADULT ONES

Land Larks #2

Back in 1626, a tribe of native American Indians called the Canarsees occupied a piece of land. The Dutch wanted this plot, and apparently offered them a selection of trinkets – whatever the equivalent of a seventeenth century fake Rolex was – which the Canarsees gratefully accepted in exchange. These baubles were probably only worth a few hundred dollars in today's money.

The section of land in question is now known as Manhattan. And its estimated present worth? About a trillion dollars, give or take a few nickels. Perhaps that's where the not-so-politically-correct term Red Indians sprang from – their embarrassed faces at negotiating what must be, hands down, the worst real-estate deal ever.

Whisky in the Tip Jar

In 2005, a rich businessman purchased a bottle of Dalmore 62-year-old single Highland malt scotch whisky, for him and some friends to enjoy at a hotel bar. It's said that he even gave the bar manager a glass, which only sounds mildly generous. Until you realize he forked out for what must be one of the most expensive rounds in history, a princely £32,000 for the highly prized Dalmore malt. Most people would have to take out a mortgage to buy a miniature of the stuff.

Wet Wheat

Before he went bankrupt, a farmer managed to obtain some £156,000 in government and EU subsidies for (amongst other things) growing crops in a field that didn't exist. When checked, the land he was claiming for was found to be located somewhere in the North Atlantic. I've heard of fish farms, but that's just ridiculous.

An Exceedingly Expensive Cake

In 2005, a Tokyo pastry chef baked one of the most expensive cakes ever. It was a fruit cake, the surface of which was laced with diamonds, making its value an estimated $1.65 million. A pointlessly expensive exercise? Yes, because in the case of this dessert, you can only have your cake and look at it. Well you certainly wouldn't consider eating it – not unless you wanted to be picking through your shit with a fine tooth comb the next morning.

Hart Felt

Moss Hart made a £2 million fortune from shows such as My Fair Lady. By the time he died he'd spent most of it on luxurious living. Exactly what you'd expect from the man who wrote "You can't take it with you."

Casino Sue

A lawyer for 9/11 victims became addicted to gambling, and was charged with siphoning money from her clients' accounts to help feed her compulsion. Apparently she eventually lost close to $1 million ($130,000 of which is said to have been stolen from clients). Like a true legal eagle, she then decided to try and sue the casinos for $20 million, for their failure to notice her gambling problem and stop her playing. The suit was dismissed in 2008, which is probably a good thing as if it had succeeded there would be quite a number of people featured in this very book stampeding towards their nearest legal practice...

Ale Money

The Beer.com domain name sold for $7 million in 2004. A sobering amount to discover on your credit card the next morning. If you're going to spend that much money on a web address you really should be hoping for sex.com at the end of the evening.

Kissing Ass

A former basketball player is well known for his high-rolling gambling. He's reputedly lost something in the order of $10 million to the house. He also once lost a bet to a basketball pundit that meant he had to kiss his ass on TV. And when the pundit brought a donkey into the studio, good as his word, the former player kissed its butt.

BLACKJACK (WHICH IS ALSO KNOWN AS PONTOON AND OR TWENTY-ONE) OFFERS A HOUSE EDGE OF JUST 0.5% MAKING IT ONE OF THE BEST CASINO PUNTS

Bust-O-Gram

In 1922, before Walt Disney hit the big time, he had a far less successful animation studio called Laugh-O-Gram. Purchased with money made from showing his cartoons at the local theatre, Walt's company got off to a good start, netting a lucrative contract. But then the firm they were dealing with went bust, and Disney soon lost all his money. Broke, with expensive overheads, he ended up sleeping in the office for a while, before eventually filing for bankruptcy. It was while sharing crumbs with a tame mouse it's said he came up with the idea for the character which was to change his life. (Quite how that gave him the idea for Oswald the Lucky Rabbit is anyone's guess).

Getting Fruity #1

In 2005, police allegedly spent £10,000 on directing a plane, a helicopter and a squad car to gather photographic evidence against a nursery nurse who'd been spotted eating an apple while driving. After ten court appearances she was reportedly fined just £60. Now if she'd been chomping a banana, it might have been more justifiable. At least then they could have sold the pics to a dodgy magazine to recoup some of the expense.

THE DUNES HOTEL AND CASINO WAS THE FIRST OPERATION TO OFFER A TOPLESS SHOW IN LAS VEGAS IN 1957

Zell's Bells

U.S. real-estate mogul Sam Zell apparently bit off more than he could chew when he bought up Tribune Co. (publisher of the *Chicago Tribune*). The company filed for bankruptcy in December 2008 with $13 billion in debt – which is quite a loss on paper, or indeed newspaper. Doubtless it prompted more than a few people to ask what the Sam Zell was going on.

Gray Expectations

In 1907, Louis McDaniel of Baltimore went to see a fight in New York. "Wonderful pugilist" Jack Gray of Texas was scheduled to take on an unknown fighter who Louis was duped into backing for $2,500. The fight took place in a hotel dining room (presumably not while people were eating), and the unknown lost. Except it was a fake fight, with fake bets and the only real loser was Louis. Still, hopefully he got a good table.

Getting Fruity #2

Would you pay $5,200 for a melon? That's the price a Japanese man was happy to part with to secure a rare Yubari melon at auction in May 2009. And that's after price deflation has been factored in – in 2008 the highest Yubari bid was a corking $25,000. And let's face it, there's nothing worse than a deflated melon (just ask any woman who has accidentally punctured her silicone implants).

Rags to Riches to Rags

Nicholas Dandolos was one of the most famous high-rollers of the gambling world. He was better known as Nick the Greek (a nickname which quite possibly got him chucked in prison a few times). In 1949, Nick took on Johnny Moss in a marathon head-to-head poker match which was played over five months (presumably not at one sitting).

The end of the game arrived when Nick was down by several million dollars, and he uttered the famous words: "Mr Moss, I have to let you go." (To the toilet, presumably, I'll bet he was bursting). Nick boasted he went from rags to riches 70 times in his life, and he won and lost a staggering estimated half a billion dollars over his career. He died near penniless.

Go On Put It In

An old former professional sportsman has led something of a colourful off-pitch life. His addictions to drink, drugs and gambling are well-documented, though it was the latter demon he found hardest to exorcise. Stories abound of him wagering up to £30,000 on a single event. Bizarrely, he was asked to be involved in a bookmaker's advertising campaign, although when the firm in question received numerous complaints they dropped the idea.

Junior Construction Set

A New Zealand woman who took a nap after buying some toys online for her 3-year-old awoke to discover the young girl had made a bid for a toy of her own. The purchase, a giant earth-moving digger, put a massive NZD$20,000 hole in the surprised mum's finances. Fortunately the woman managed to cancel the sale, although that put her daughter's tender for a new car park in serious doubt.

A Girl's Best Friend

In 2006, a jeweller bought a diamond for $7.5 million. It wasn't big, shiny and impressive though. It was the diamond.com web domain. Your girlfriend would be the one bringing you down with one knee (to the bollocks) if you proposed with that.

Max Not-So-Well

Media tycoon Robert Maxwell reportedly managed quite an impressive quick-losing gambling feat. He's alleged to have lost £1.5 million in three minutes playing three roulette wheels simultaneously. The only thing the average man can lose 1.5 million of in three minutes involves an ensuing pregnancy.

Family Misfortune #2

An American man who scooped a $16 million lottery jackpot in 1988 wasn't feeling too lucky by the time his nearest and dearest had finished with him. His former landlady sued him, claiming they had agreed to split the winnings, and a judge forced him to hand over a third of the money. He was also badgered by family into investing in car and restaurant businesses which didn't return a profit, and one brother allegedly hired a hitman to kill him to grab the potential inheritance. Other large sums were frittered away on daft luxuries like a twin-engine plane which he couldn't fly as he had no pilot's license. According to reports he ended up living on $450 a month and food stamps, although at least he didn't have to worry about snipers and lawsuits any more.

Waste of InfoSpace

In 2000, a Nebraska woman looking for somewhere to invest her retirement savings decided to purchase InfoSpace stock, based on glowing reports from numerous financial analysts. The company seemed like a safe bet so she ploughed everything she had into it – some $40,000 – and waited for the profits to roll in. The profits, however, rolled out. She didn't lose everything when the dot-com bubble burst, thankfully, but retiring on the remaining $1,450 might have been difficult...

THE KING OF CLUBS ORIGINALLY REPRESENTED ALEXANDER THE GREAT

Ruby Slip-up

When Wrekin Construction went bust in 2009 owing approximately £20.7 million there was at least some comfort to be had in knowing that the company wasn't entirely penniless. Its chief asset, the "Gem of Tanzania", was a 2kg uncut ruby worth approximately £11 million. At least that's what the valuation certificate said. Unfortunately, the valuation certificate turned out to be a fake. The exact value of the gem couldn't be immediately determined, but the ruby certainly wasn't worth enough to get the company out of the red.

Fennessy's Whiskey

In 1882, seasoned drinker Fennessy placed a £5 bet that he could drink six glasses of whiskey in 60 seconds. It was a challenge he'd managed before and his endeavour drew a sizeable crowd, with plenty of side wagers. He downed the first five without problem, but then keeled over and died. Fennessy had so much alcohol in his system it was suggested at his post mortem that crushing him like a grape would produce a particularly potent vintage. Yeah, not to mention splatting blood and guts everywhere.

THE KING OF DIAMONDS ORIGINALLY REPRESENTED JULIUS CAESAR

Houston We Have a Problem

Everyone has surely heard of Enron, the Houston-based energy firm which *Fortune* magazine named America's most innovative company for six years running. Unfortunately Enron's major "innovation" turned out to be its accounting, the truth of which was uncovered in 2001 when huge losses were found hidden in offshore vehicles. Financial ones, not boats.

A massive scandal ensued, and several Enron executives were jailed. The figure put on Enron's investor losses varies from source to source, but is generally estimated to be around the $70 to $80 billion mark. It would probably have been cheaper to keep America warm simply by burning the cash.

Bit of a Pisser

Ever wondered what the world's most costliest piss was? Me neither, but an employee at Yellowstone National Park who took a leak into Old Faithful must be right up there. The geezer was fired – not Old Faithful, the man – and apparently also fined $750. And now you also know how Yellowstone Park got its name.

Piano Plonkers

A grand piano given to an art dealer by John Lennon shortly before his death was reportedly sold for £2,000 by mistake. It was worth an estimated £1 million. Imagine that.

THE KING OF HEARTS WAS ORIGINALLY KING CHARLEMAGNE

Skip Time

The agent of a well-known player bet the footballer that he couldn't kick a ball from the roof of a building into a skip on the ground across the way. The wager was for the agent's £15,000 watch, which he lost when the ball hit the skip bang on target. The actual footage of the event is on YouTube, although there's the chance that the video's a rubbish fake.

Spread Batting

1999 saw a spread betting company bowl itself something of a bouncer. While pricing up markets for the Cricket World Cup, the firm's sports analysts neglected to account for the effect the white cricket ball would have on the English game. This meant they wildly underestimated the number of wides that would be bowled over the 42 games, thinking it would be 245-265. Fans knew bowlers would have difficulty controlling the white ball's swing, and fell over themselves to place bets above that spread. 979 wides were eventually bowled, and apparently the company lost £500,000. How's that for a sticky betting wicket...

Sold The Farm

In the 1960s, an unnamed member of the House of Lords reportedly gambled away a fortune playing roulette. While most of us would be thinking of slitting our wrists, he took the financial hit more nonchalantly, calmly proclaiming "I suppose I shall have to sell off some of my outlying farms." So still sell farming really, just of a kind not involving a razor blade.

Jumper

A Chinese man financed a construction project that failed, leaving him with a 2 million yuan ($293,000) debt. Seeing no way out, he climbed onto the Haizhu Bridge and told passers-by he was going to jump. Five hours later, he was still talking about it so a bored motorist got out of his car, walked over and shoved the ditherer off the bridge (he landed on an air cushion below and survived). That's the sort of decision making that would have got the man's construction plans off the ground floor.

You What?

The Las Vegas County Association of the Deaf spent over three years raising $270,000 for a convention, but then the bank holding it went bust. The organisers wouldn't have needed lip reading skills to know what the contributors said when they discovered that $170,000 of their money wasn't insured.

THE COLOUR "DOBBER" THAT BINGO PLAYERS PREFER IS APPARENTLY PURPLE

Oh Doctor!

A wealthy doctor managed to blow his £1.5 million fortune on luxurious living. He had a string of lovers, all of whom he treated to expensive gifts. He gave one girlfriend a £1,000 watch, even though he couldn't recall her name. A diamond-encrusted ID bracelet might have been a more useful choice.

Premium Bonds

In 1990, a London financial messenger was robbed at knifepoint in the street. The mugger (who'd been put up to it by an organized crime syndicate) made off with £292 million in treasury bonds. The victim's bosses probably wanted to revive an old tradition when they found out the bad news – shooting the messenger.

Fat Fingers

A New Zealand bank teller processed a man's temporary NZD$100,000 overdraft and accidentally put a decimal point in the wrong place. The man, realising he now had NZD$10 million in the bank, decided to take the money and run (well NZD$3.8 million of it anyway). The clumsy teller was issued with a written warning. Hopefully the full stops were in all the right places.

Sea-Saw

In 1764, a sailor won a hefty wager and put his winnings in his jacket pocket. Getting ready to take shore leave he decided to spend some of his good fortune on a new jacket, and so tossed the old one into the sea. It was only as he stood watching it disappearing beneath the waves it dawned on him where the money was. I've heard of splashing the cash, but that's ridiculous.

Jack Loot

Actor/comedian Jack Benny once asked a man to (illegally) import a gold bracelet and two diamond clasps into America. Customs found out about the arrangement and took Benny to court. He admitted smuggling the jewellery, which was worth $1,400, and was fined $10,000. Benny used to perform a sketch in which he went down to a vault that was protected by a moat with crocodiles, a guard and chains. He was lucky he didn't end up serving time in there.

Extreme Makeover

A Mississippi woman discovered that the plot of land next to her house had been acquired by the local university (with a view to expansion) when she returned from a day out to find contractors hard at work – demolishing her home. The University said it was possible that pranksters had switched the signs around. Tsk... Students, eh?

DICE WERE TRADITIONALLY CARVED FROM ANIMAL BONES

Fat Chance

Fouad Al-Zayat is nicknamed the "Fat Man" in gambling circles, and this whale – someone who always bets at least $1 million – has certainly laid down some porking great wagers. The Syrian reportedly lost around £23 million at a Mayfair casino over a period of 12 years, which might make a lesser man's wallet thinner, but not this billionaire's. It's made of whale-skin, presumably.

No Buyers

In 1922, Jack Cohen bet his friend William Wolf $200 that he could sell $50 worth of silver half dollars for a quarter each in fifteen minutes. Wolf believed New Yorkers would be too suspicious to take up the bargain, but Cohen was confident. Unfortunately, he failed to find a single buyer in his allotted time, was moved on by the police on several occasions, and eventually arrested and fined $2 for trying to sell items without a license. When he tried to pay the fine with four of his coins the court clerk bit into one to check its validity.

Munch Bunch

Two Edvard Munch paintings, worth an estimated £50 million, were stolen from an Oslo museum in 2004. The owners failed to insure them against theft, which must have made them want to scream.

THE OLDEST KNOWN SET OF DICE WERE MADE FROM CLAY AND ARE THOUGHT TO BE SOME 5,000 YEARS OLD

The Not-so Great Caruso

The famous Italian opera singer Enrico Caruso went to Paris in 1908 to get over a failed romance. While there he bemoaned to a friend he was almost anonymous in the city. His friend laughed at the idea that The Great Caruso could go unrecognized for so much as an hour and a wager was struck. The friend lost comprehensively. No one paid any attention at all to the singer, and they couldn't even get the waiter to look in their direction – although that's a pretty standard reaction in most posh French eateries even today.

Spit Me Baby, One More Time

In 2004, a piece of gum alleged to have been chewed and spat out by Britney Spears sold for $14,000 on eBay. The seller reportedly pushed the price up by bidding against himself. Hopefully it wasn't toxic.

Brown, Moist and Steaming

Kopi Luwak, the most expensive coffee in the world, is made from coffee beans eaten, passed through the digestive tract and then excreted by the Asian palm civet. It sells for up to $600 a pound, or $50 a cup. Which, it has to be said, is a lot of money for freshly brewed weasel shit.

Lost in La Mancha

In 2000, Terry Gilliam began work on *The Man Who Killed Don Quixote*. Financed by European money-makers, he had a $32 million budget to play around with. Unfortunately jets roaring overhead made it impossible to hear the actors, a flash flood caused chaos and the man who played Don Quixote developed a spinal problem that prevented him from sitting on a horse. The film was eventually abandoned but it wasn't a total loss. They managed to get a couple of minutes of decent footage – unusual for a Terry Gilliam film.

Cover Charge

Sir Peter Blake designed the Beatles' iconic *Sergeant Pepper's Lonely Hearts Club Band* album cover and was paid just £200 for his work and the copyright to it. He could have asked for more but frankly who'd have thought an album by the biggest band in the world would have been so popular?

Taxing Times

In the 1960s, a young gambler who won £70,000 playing Baccarat Chemin de Fer in a London club went home jubilantly to his wife, only to be told off for not getting a tax receipt. He returned to the club to collect the receipt but while there started gambling again and lost all of his winnings, plus an additional £110,000. At least he no longer had to worry about the tax problem.

CASINO DICE HAVE AN ABSOLUTELY EQUAL CHANCE OF LANDING ON ANY ONE SIDE DUE TO THEIR PRECISION MANUFACTURE

Football Crazy #2

George Reynolds made a £300 million fortune from manufacturing kitchen worktops and invested some £27 million in Darlington Football Club. Most of the money went towards building a new stadium (presumably not out of MDF). But then his business collapsed, and the club went into administration before being sold off for £1 million. Somewhat bizarrely it's said that George had no interest at all in football. Which is presumably why he invested in Darlington.

Kicking Up a Stink

A former deputy head teacher took her old school to court alleging constructive dismissal and sexual discrimination, and seeking £1 million in damages. Apparently her bosses had failed to replace her chair which made a farting noise when she sat in it. She lost the case and presumably responded by making a loud raspberry when told of the outcome.

Toxic Lady

Erin Brockovich lost a reported $1 million on a house which turned out to be infested with a slimy black mould. Julia Roberts, who won a Best Actress Oscar in 2001 for playing her in a movie, has somewhat surprisingly yet to express an interest in returning for Erin Brockovich: The Fungus Years.

Charity Begins At The Racetrack

A senior welfare officer for a Jewish charity forgot to lock his desk before going on holiday. By chance someone happened to look inside and discovered the absent worker had been embezzling money on and off for 13 years. When he arrived back at work he was arrested and admitted gambling away nearly £24,000. He was jailed for seven years. What you'd call the luck of the drawer.

Airport Stanley

In 1982, the Falklands War put the tiny South Atlantic islands on the map and three years later the bleak, sparsely inhabited corner that was forever England got its own international airport at a cost of some £400 million. Given there's only 3,100 or so inhabitants on the island, and half a million sheep, that was a "baamy" extravagance. Of course, maybe it was built for the Falklands' woolly inhabitants. Just because pigs don't fly... (Mind you, I wouldn't want to be the airport official in charge of counting them through the gate).

Family Misfortune #3

A bank manager fuelled his gambling addiction by plundering £15,000 from bank accounts belonging to his wife, uncle and mother-in-law. That's taking the phrase "keeping it in the family" a little too literally.

Serious Spending

In 1985, a famous singer's brother went bust after a series of unsuccessful investments. The inheritance he'd hoped to get from his mother failed to materialise, leaving him without so much as half a sixpence to his name.

Blew It

A wealthy businessman spent £493,000 of his company's money on a £1,000-a-night escort. Obsessed, he bought her expensive gifts and took her on luxury holidays. When the fraud was discovered, his firm went bust with a loss of some 170 jobs. He was clearly a grade-A sucker and, having been able to get that much money out of him, she clearly must have been as well.

I'm So Not Excited

An Internet portal along the same lines as Yahoo and Netscape, Excite was one of the big early dot-com movers and shakers. Despite having lost millions the year before, it was snapped up by @Home Network in January 1999 for a whopping $6.7 billion. The merger led to the company being awkwardly renamed Excite@Home. Unfortunately the stock collapsed within 18 months, losing 90% of its value. A year later the firm was bankrupt and the staff became UnemployedSittingAround@Home.

ACCORDING TO A 2008 SURVEY, OVER 70% OF AMERICANS BELIEVE DEBT IS AN INEVITABLE PART OF THEIR WAY OF LIFE

Back for More

A Japanese tourist hitchhiking his way across Alaska in 2007 set up camp for the evening, went for a short walk and returned to discover everything he owned had been stolen. He managed to contact his parents who wired him money so he could start again. A few days later he met a man in a truck who told him he knew where the stolen gear was. Trustingly he got in the vehicle and was driven out into the woods, where he was knocked unconscious and robbed again. By the same guy who'd stolen his camping gear originally.

Handicapped Play

When a champion golfer lost a play-off at the World Championships, he did what any sane sportsman would do. Picked himself up, dusted himself off, and drove all the way to Las Vegas where he proceeded to blow $1.5 million on slot machines at $5,000 a time. Forget birdies, eagles and albatrosses, he struck a dodo there.

Having gambled away somewhere between $50 and $60 million over the years, he should probably think about buying some trousers with reinforced pockets. His money is clearly burning a hole in one of them.

Tarred and Leathered

They say it's not what you know, it's who you know. And in 1899, the police force of Cincinnati knew a man who owned a racehorse. Dr Tarr, the horse, not the owner, had romped home in a couple of previous races. So when the owner started boasting that "the Doctor was fit to win" a large proportion of the police, and some City Hall officials decided to back him, disguising themselves or crossing the river to Kentucky to place the bets in secret. So popular was the horse with the officials, it quickly became the favourite. Unfortunately for its backers, Dr Tarr placed nowhere, leaving the boys in blue feeling very blue indeed.

Van Didn't Gogh

A gang who spent months carefully planning to steal Van Gogh paintings worth £130 million from the National Gallery in London were arrested when they were spotted trying to free the clamped getaway vehicle. They'd already spent £100,000 of the money they were anticipating from the haul, which made the double yellow lines on the road a pretty costly piece of painting in itself.

Chet bets

Fulvio Chester Forte Jr, Chet to his friends, was the first director of *Monday Night Football* on ABC Sports in the 1960s. He loved sports so much he gambled away nearly $4 million and a million dollar home betting on them. Clearly winning was not his forte.

IN 2008, SOME 40,000 HOMES WERE REPOSSESSED IN THE UK

Emperor Norton

Joshua Abraham Norton was born in London in 1818 but made a fortune from the Californian gold rush, and by 1853 was worth an estimated $250,000. When a famine hit China, leading to a ban on the export of rice, Norton decided he could control the market by buying up a boat load of the stuff from Peru. Unfortunately for him, South America had an almost unlimited supply, and his gamble failed to pay off. A few years later he was declared bankrupt but after a short self-imposed exile, he returned and proclaimed himself Norton I, Emperor of the United States. And issued his own money.

Crock Around the Clock

Warren Harding was the President of the United States in the early 1920s. He is said to have been a chancer who enjoyed hosting all-night poker games at the White House, although apparently he wasn't very good at cards. One story holds that he lost china in a poker session. Not the country, mind, but the White House crockery which apparently dated back to the presidency of Benjamin Harrison.

Pub Plunderer

In 2006, a landlord stole £11,800 from the pub where he worked (which shall remain nameless) and "plough"-ed it into horse racing. Unlike the nags he was backing, the chap had form. He'd previously gambled away another £8,000 from a different pub.

GLEN CHORNY WON THE EUROPEAN POKER TOUR IN 2008, SCOOPING OVER $3 MILLION

Ghost Busters

A Japanese man and his eight disciples conned thousands of gullible people out of millions of yen by telling them they had spirits of dead people attached to their bodies. One passer-by at a train station was told she had the spirit of a dead man with severed legs clinging to her waist. (A fare-dodger by the sounds of it). They were then offered a costly exorcism. When arrested the chief spooksman told the police officer it wasn't fraud, it was a gift. And that he himself was possessed by the dead spirit of Marcel Marceau. Well I think that's what he claimed anyway. He mimed the last part using only amusing hand gestures.

Bank Error In Your Favour

In 2001, an Irish man asked his bank to convert IR£1,500 into pesetas and transfer it into his Spanish bank account. A mix-up meant he was accidentally credited with 316,900 Euros, instead of pesetas, a tidy £250,000 windfall. He was able to withdraw a chunk of the cash before the bank realized, and refused to give it back. The bank froze his account and took him to court to recover the outstanding amount. The actual outcome was never reported, but it's safe to assume he didn't earn any interest.

AT THE CLOSE OF 2008, OVER 200,000 UK BORROWERS WERE MORE THAN 3 MONTHS BEHIND WITH MORTGAGE PAYMENTS

Street Race

The Earl of Barrymore was a young, fit and quick man, so he was very confident about winning when he was challenged to a hundred yard dash by an obese middle-aged butcher for a sizeable wager (the exact amount wasn't recorded). He even agreed to the butcher's demands for a 35 yard head-start, and also let him pick the course. The canny butcher chose Black Lion Lane, one of the narrowest streets in England. When the race began the Earl caught up to him very quickly, but there was simply no room to pass the cheating fat bastard, who must have been laughing his chops off as he went on to win.

Soapy Flit Yank

Jefferson Randolph Smith was an Alaskan con artist of the nineteenth century. Over many years he cheated countless unsuspecting folks out of hundreds of bucks by selling what were apparently bars of soap with dollar bills wrapped around them. The money was inserted in full view of the crowd, and then an accomplice in the throng would "buy" one and win.

Gullible members of the public would then pile in to spend a buck a bar, hoping to bag the $100 which was supposedly wrapped inside one. Of course, all the moneyed bars were cunningly switched so nobody but his fellow con-men plants won anything. "Soapy" Smith, as he became known, would then make a clean getaway with all their cash.

Olive a Cheeseburger

Another poker player proposition bet, this time a food related one involving pros Howard Lederer (a vegetarian) and David Grey (who hates olives). Grey bet Lederer he wouldn't eat a cheeseburger for $10,000. Lederer happily wolfed one down, which was one expensive not-so-happy meal for Grey. Worse still, Lederer gave him the opportunity to win his money back if he just ate three olives, but he refused. He must really hate olives.

Hat's That Then

In the late nineteenth century, George Lingard succeeded in losing his wife's entire fortune, some $50,000, on Wall Street. To solve their financial problems he started forging cheques – very successfully at first. The fraud was eventually uncovered and Lingard went on the run. When the police caught up with him he almost managed to convince them that they had the wrong man – until a detective removed Lingard's hat and found his name written on the lining inside. Reports at the time aren't clear whether his underpants were similarly labelled.

Uninsured

The Northern Bank in Belfast was robbed in 2004. The gang got away with an estimated £26.4 million, which was insured by the bank itself. I'll bet that was an interesting claim.

Fresh Prince

In 1922, Prince Murat, a descendent of one of Napoleon's Generals, went to court to prevent his son, Prince Jerome Murat, from spending any more money. Murat junior had managed to burn through a million francs in four years. His father felt his son was far too young to make proper financial decisions and wanted the court to treat him as a minor in money matters. Junior probably wasn't overly impressed, seeing as he was 30 at the time.

Stop! Hammer Time

Rapper MC Hammer amassed a $33 million dollar fortune thanks to the success of mega-selling albums such as *Please Hammer Don't Hurt Em*, yet still couldn't afford a decent pair of trousers which fitted properly. He reportedly spent $12 million of his riches on a crib in California (that's one very expensive cot), and used the rest for other essential rap-star items such as a fleet of cars, a couple of helicopters, some racehorses and an expensive entourage of 300 or so paid hangers-on.

The hits soon dried up though, and faced with debts of $13 million he filed for bankruptcy and his home went under the hammer. Because the water was cut off poor old MCH didn't even get to use his expensive gold toilet one final time. As his wife explained, "You can't flush this." (Possibly.)

Car Trouble

A German man who was planning to buy an Audi A3 cabriolet took it for a test drive on the autobahn. His foot was down, the roof was down, the breeze was in his hair and he was feeling good. Right up until the point when a strong gust of wind blew the envelope containing 23,000 Euros clean off the back seat, showering the motorists behind with the money he'd intended to use to buy the car. That's certainly one way to blow a fortune.

Rail Plonker #1

In 2007, a man travelling on a train from London to Kent had a nagging feeling he'd left something behind when he walked out of his destination station. And he had – a white paper bag containing expensive jewellery and watches. "Irreplaceable items" as he later described them (although not "unforgettable" obviously). British transport police failed to find any trace of the missing bag, although a tramp wearing a Rolex said he saw a suspicious looking character going "that way."

Rockingham Horse Shit

In 1780, the Marquess of Rockingham, Charles Watson-Wentworth, supposedly bet an anonymous party that he could drive a coach and horses through the eye of a needle. As we all know, it's tricky enough to get a camel through one, let alone four horses and a carriage. Having arranged the wager, Charles built a 45 foot high sandstone structure shaped like a needle, with a gap in the bottom he could drive through. Needless to say, the chap on the other side of the wager probably wasn't too impressed, but had to fork out. No wonder rich men don't get into Heaven, not when they make unsporting bets like this.

A Charity Case

A Northumberland man who'd built up a multi-million pound fortune from scratch, including a stately home/hotel on a ten-acre estate, came to the conclusion that if money can't buy you happiness it should at least be able to rent it for someone else. He put the lot up for sale, with every penny of the proceeds earmarked for charity. "You can't take it with you when go," he observed. Tell that to the Pharaohs.

TOTAL UK PERSONAL DEBT STOOD AT ALMOST £1.46 TRILLION IN MARCH 2009, EXCEEDING THE COUNTRY'S GROSS DOMESTIC PRODUCT

Sony and Yet So Far

The economic downturn hit a lot of companies hard, but Japanese electronics manufacturers suffered more than most. Sony reported a loss of $1 billion for the fiscal year ending in March 2009, a deficit made all the more impressive considering the company had posted a profit of $3.8 billion the previous year. Still, there was some good news for Sony – I hear a new landfill site has opened up near Tokyo. Maybe if the company asks them nicely they'll be willing to find a home for all of those unsold PS3s...

My, My, Macpherson

Mimi Macpherson, sister of Australian supermodel Elle, was declared bankrupt in 2008 with reported debts of AUD$300,000 (nearly two thirds of which she allegedly owed to her father). Elle is known as "The Body." With financial skills like that it's clear Mimi isn't "The Brains."

Paint Shop

A vendor who sold forged paintings on eBay was arrested in 2007, after police estimated he made around $200,000 from various deluded bidders who apparently thought they were purchasing Picasso originals and suchlike. According to a detective who caught him by posing as a customer, the painting he purchased arrived with a smudge of wet paint on the back, still smelling of oil. Not so much a master forger as a masturbator.

Big Numbers Plate #1

In 2008, a stockbroker from Dubai paid out $14 million for a personalised license plate, the largest amount ever recorded. The plate number: Simply "1". What car he used this preposterously expensive plate on isn't clear, but let's hope he did something ironic and slapped it on a Ford Fiesta.

Brothers Grim

In 1905, when Thomas Powell died in hospital he at least had the comfort of knowing that his two brothers would profit from his death thanks to a recent £7,000 win on a local sweepstake. It was fortunate for him in one way (although clearly not another) that he died when he did as his brothers, anticipating living the rest of their lives in relative luxury, would probably have killed him after discovering he'd failed to pay the sweepstake fee, and so hadn't actually won anything.

Dig For Poverty

In 1932, John George Tanner finally achieved his dream. After years of scrimping and saving, managing to put aside the majority of his meagre wage every week, while he, his mother and his disabled sister survived on the remainder, he was at last in a position to buy the smallholding he'd always wanted. His hard work, and their hardship didn't pay off though and he went bust three years later. What you'd call putting your family in farm's way.

Shedding a Fortune

An American inventor who made millions from his ideas and bought himself a sizeable ranch, lost everything in the Great Depression and was forced to move into smaller accommodation. Speaking of his change in circumstances he said, "I am penniless, but content." Sentiments that, coming from a man reduced to living in a former cowshed, certainly deserve a big pat on the back.

Couldn't Afford It

When Henry Ford was looking to make it big in the automobile industry (at that point more of an automobile workshop) he asked a young British officer to help back his venture. The man was keen, but his wife felt the investment – which would have involved re-mortgaging their house – sounded too risky to be worth it. A wrong turn that meant they missed out on future millions.

Mad Money

When a media tycoon divorced his wife in the late 90s, the exact settlement figure remained a mystery, although one source alleged that it was the most expensive divorce in history at the cost of over $1 billion of assets. Whatever the true amount was, you can bet it was a sizeable sum that would have Heather Mills kicking herself in comparison (a task easier for her than most people).

A QUARTER OF AMERICANS ADMIT TO HAVING PARTAKEN OF ILLEGAL GAMBLING AT SOME POINT IN THEIR LIVES

Creesed Up

Alfred Creese was one of the greatest inventors of the early twentieth century. Amongst other things he invented the monoplane, the first self-starter motorcar, pneumatic shock absorbers and expanding airplane wings. Unfortunately while rival inventors made a fortune from the same ideas, he just lost everything trying to get a single one of his to fly. Surprising really, particularly in the case of the monoplane.

Who Wants To Be A Milinaire

Kitty Milinaire inherited a vast fortune from her father when she was 25 and, with millions in the bank, went on to live the high life throughout the 1970s. But then she developed a taste for gambling which turned into an uncontrollably gluttony. She gambled away her fortune, blew her £260,000 overdraft and was forced to flog off much of her jewellery. She even sold her Paris apartment then wagered and lost the £95,000 she got for it. After three years there was nothing left in the Kitty, and she went from being a real-life Pussy Galore to a Moggy Not-Much, eventually being forced to file for bankruptcy.

IN "LET IT RIDE", A VARIATION OF POKER PLAYED AGAINST THE CASINO RATHER THAN OTHER PLAYERS, THE HOUSE EDGE IS 3.5%

All Bar Nun

The singing nun, Jeanine Deckers (aka Sister Smile), found fame in the 1960s with the song 'Dominique'. It made her an estimated £250,000 which, when the tax man came calling at least, she claimed to have given away to her convent. It all ended tragically when, broke and hooked on drugs in the 1980s, Sister Smile committed suicide with her lesbian lover. Sounds like convent life wasn't really her thing.

Big Mama

The yomama.com domain name was sold for $17,650 in May 2009, a purchase that could easily spin out its own insult. "Yo Mama is so fat people jog around her for exercise!" "Yeah, well, Yo Mama is so stupid she'd spend over $17,000 on a useless domain name."

Sister Act

A dentist died of a broken heart two years after his sister passed away. Dr Thomas Burgh quit his lucrative job, frittered away his fortune, and became a recluse. He still treated the occasional patient, but only ones who couldn't afford to pay him. He had been utterly devoted to his sister who he'd lived with for 21 years up until the time of her death. It was rumoured they weren't actually blood relatives though, so maybe she received a good few fillings from her brother, and not in the dentist chair...

LAS VEGAS IS ALSO KNOWN AS "SIN CITY"

Monster Drive

Back in the 1930s, an American golfer bet some fellow players $1,000 that he could drive a ball over 500 yards. A feat that even today would leave Tiger Woods open-mouthed. They agreed, thinking that distance was impossible, but his highly confident club mates actually lost their stake. What he didn't tell them was that he was going to take the drive on the shore of a frozen lake, where it skidded on a hell of a long way. Bet they were really teed off.

Left Behind

A customer walked into a bank with $1,000 of cash inside a white envelope, intending to purchase a cashier's cheque. While filling in the forms he suddenly remembered he'd left something important at home, so walked out of the bank, leaving the money behind. Never mind a cashier's cheque, I'll bet he made a pants deposit when he realized what he'd done and returned to find it gone. CCTV showed another customer taking it – presumably an honest mistake. After all one unattended white envelope stuffed with cash looks much like another.

Dry Rot

In 1885, the wife of a wealthy dry goods merchant took her neighbour to court, seeking $5,000 in damages for "alienating her husband's affection." Mrs Renker claimed that since the woman's arrival, her husband had let his business go to ruin and had squandered the entire family fortune in six months. Sounds like he was fed up of dry goods and wanted something a little fresher.

Financially Misadvised

A financial advisor who failed to set up an insurance policy for a client stole thousands of pounds from his building society employer to cover a claim. When the client was diagnosed with leukaemia, the advisor reportedly paid the £175 a month critical illness cover himself. He began stealing more from the building society to compensate people who had lost money on his advice, and then started to steal from richer clients to compensate the company. Inevitably, everything collapsed and he was arrested. The defending solicitor described his client as a Robin Hood-type figure. The Judge, thinking more along the lines of a Robin Bastard-type figure, sentenced the hapless ex-advisor to 14 months.

THE WALL STREET CRASH OF 1929 SAW A FALL OF 13% IN THE MARKET, FOLLOWED BY A FURTHER 11% THE NEXT WEEK

School Sums

A finance officer working at a Welsh school decided she deserved a bonus and wrote several cheques to herself, carefully forging the headmaster's signature. Over the course of a year she stole £55,00, and spent it all on anything which took her fancy, including a laptop and digital camera. After being caught she was admitted to hospital with OCD. Or a variant of it anyway – TTD possibly. Thieving Twat Disease.

An Organised Career

Alfred Lamport built up a sizeable fortune in business and decided to retire early. He speculated some money on the stock market, then some more, until eventually by 1910 he'd lost the lot. Fortunately, when things were at their grimmest, a new opportunity opened up for Alfred in the music business. It was repetitive work, with a high turnover and some frequent monkey business, but at least his job as an organ-grinder allowed him to eat.

AFTER THE WALL STREET CRASH OF 1929, THE U.S. STOCK MARKET SLID DOWNWARDS UNTIL 90% OF ITS VALUE HAD BEEN LOST IN 1932

Weeping And Grailing

When *The Da Vinci Code* became a massive worldwide phenomenon, author Dan Brown wasn't the only one to profit from it. Michael Baigent and Richard Leigh saw sales of their similar earlier work, *The Holy Blood and the Holy Grail*, increase massively too. Rather than being pleased with the unexpected profit, they decided to take Brown to court for plagiarism (and, just possibly, to make some easy extra dosh). They lost the case and found themselves saddled with a – Holy Shit and Holy Christ – £3 million legal bill.

Flower Power

In just 20 months, between January 1996 and September 1997, a pop celebrity apparently managed to spend his way through £30 million. £9.6 million of that went on property, which is fair enough, but he also shelled out a colossal £293,000 just on flowers. When asked about the extravagance, he said, "I like flowers." Yeah, there's liking them, and then there's spending close to £300,000 on a shed-load of the petal-headed bastards.

Mother of an Invention

Susan Schintz was a very wealthy woman in the 1920s with around £400,000 in liquid assets, another £390,000 in trust and an estate. Needing someone to look after her cars she employed Frederick Rapson. The two became very close and she started to finance his various inventions. He created an unpuncturable tyre but it only succeeded in putting a massive £200,000 hole in Schintz's finances. She became bankrupt in 1930, a tiresome affair no doubt.

Lightfooted

David Lowry le Blanc Lightfoot had a good start in life. Despite being saddled with a name like that of course. He went to Eton school and inherited a fortune of between £40,000 and £80,000. After the Second World War ended he began investing some money in theatrical shows, and four years later had spent the lot. He still had ideas though, just not the capital to back them up, so began borrowing and defrauding people. When arrested the once wealthy public schooled destitute told the police: "If people part with their money as easily as that they deserve to lose it." Well, exactly...

Cold Shoulder

American George Bacon joined the British army in 1940, keen to do his bit in the fight against Hitler. He met an English girl, married her, and they moved to Nottingham. His rich father, a Boston book publisher, was so outraged by his son's move overseas, he cut him out of his will and left his entire fortune to Harvard University for research into the common cold. A bequeath not to be sneezed at.

On Credit

At the turn of the last century, Violet Charlesworth became something of a celebrity. Claiming to be about to come into a £2 million inheritance, she went on a massive spending spree, buying up expensive jewellery and cars, renting country homes across Britain and speculating and losing large sums of money on the stock exchange. When the credit started to dry up and it became clear she'd made up the inheritance story, Violet faked her own death, arranged to be discovered again, and started a short-lived career telling her story on the stage. With no discernable talent, aside from lying, Violet's star soon faded and people quickly lost interest. Not like today of course when a total lack of talent is the one essential requirement for any young female celebrity. Well, that and a sex tape.

THE HOUSE EDGE OF SLOT MACHINES CAN BE ANYTHING BETWEEN 2% AND 15%

Spin Out

A couple in Las Vegas who had enjoyed a phenomenally good run on roulette and were $20,000 up, decided to split the winnings and gamble half each on one final spin – she picked red, while he took black. It was the ultimate battle of the sexes. Until the ball plopped into the green zero, and they lost the whole lot. I'll bet that was an uncomfortably quiet journey home.

A Banked Clone

When an American woman's beloved 17-year-old cat died she did just what any caring pet owner would do. Forked out $50,000 to have it cloned. The result was an apparently carbon copy kitty called Little Nicky which not only looked almost identical to the original but shared many similar traits, including a fondness for sleeping, cleaning, being fussed and chasing after small moving objects.

Battle Royale

In 1906, two men had a contest to see which of them could win the most money at faro and roulette. One was a bank president; the other's profession wasn't recorded. The battle went on for two days and nights until the banker was forced to admit defeat. It's not known how much better his opponent did, but it's safe to assume he probably hadn't blown an eye-watering £130,000.

CHINA'S NATIONAL LOTTERY SAW REVENUES OF $15 BILLION IN 2008

Slipped Away

Conman Sidney Alman King, known to his victims as Slippery Sid, died penniless in 1975, sixty years after committing his first crime. He built up a sizeable fortune from a fake slimming business and an "infallible" roulette system (which was infallible for him, but not for those who actually gambled on it). Despite his successes, the money soon slipped through Sid's fingers, thanks to a liking, but not a talent, for gambling.

The Mirror Cracked

A model showing off a several thousand-year-old mirror on a Chinese TV show dropped and smashed the $1 million antique. On reflection, perhaps a goalkeeper would have been a better choice to parade the piece around.

Off Like A Shot

Larry Fay was a notorious racketeer who made a fortune selling dairy produce at inflated prices in 1930s New York. Having milked the scam for as long as possible, he became a nightclub owner, but then ran into money troubles. He told a doorman at his club that the man would have to start sharing his job and wages with another bouncer. Larry's aim was to save money. His bouncer's aim was more accurate though and he promptly shot his former boss dead. A rather emphatic way of handing in your resignation.

Kiss And Don't Tell

Jerry Hall signed a £1 million publishing deal to write a tell-all autobiography in 2007. After two years of solid writing, her efforts were reportedly rejected by the publisher for focusing too much on her life and not enough on Mick Jagger's. She was introduced to some ghost writers to help her pep things up a little (removing boring stuff about herself and replacing it with salacious content about Mick probably). It didn't work out in the end though, the book was cancelled and Jerry was told she'd have to hand back the £500,000 advance.

Funny Sale

Web domain name humour.org was sold for $3,530 in 2009. The seller was probably hoping for more, but Americans looking at the name didn't get it.

Handed In A Fortune

In 1967, an unnamed New York taxi driver (unnamed because he was driving an unlicensed cab and refused to give his details) discovered a passenger had left his briefcase in the back of the cab. He handed it in at the airport and drove off with a new fare. The man who had left the case behind was understandably grateful to be reunited with it, seeing as it contained £21.4 million in negotiable promissory notes. That's what you call a big tip.

You'll Never Park Alone

A British man managed to get himself landed with an impressive parking fine to the value of £4,300. The charge was levied by the city council because he was allowing football fans to park their cars in the large grounds of his house (right next to the stadium) on match day, and charging them for the privilege. An illegal act without planning permission for a car park, and he probably had to admit, it was a fair cop.

Tipped Over The Edge

In 1969, a British punter placed a sizeable wager on a horse that a tipster had described as a "certain winner." When it failed to be first past the post, he was understandably miffed. Believing that, like the jockey, he'd been taken for a ride, he reported the tipster to the authorities, claiming the advice he'd been given had broken the Trades Description Act. The chances of his complaint succeeding didn't net very favourable odds.

Food for Thought

A supermarket worker who was throwing away a ripped bag of fruit slices popped one in his mouth as he went to the bin. Unfortunately for him, his boss spotted him chewing the bit of apple, and according to newspaper reports he was later sacked from his £12,000-a-year job for theft. Some things haven't changed much since biblical times – don't eat the forbidden fruit.

THE "MOULIN ROUGE" BECAME THE FIRST RACIALLY UNSEGREGATED LAS VEGAS HOTEL AND CASINO, IN 1955

Western Debit

In 1960, hire purchase company Western Credit was shocked to discover that it had made a £300,000 loss. The firm had recorded a £188,000 profit the previous year and things appeared to have been on the up. Investigations showed that the company had been duped into handling suspect business and had a number of entirely fictitious clients on its books. The source of the HP fraud was never reported.

Double Winner

In 1938, an unemployed waiter who claimed he'd won £30,000 in a sweepstake found people were willing to loan him items off the back of it. He managed to blag a car, clothes, a watch and two rings. He even got an advance on the winnings from his own father. When it came to light that he hadn't really won the money, the ex-waiter simply upped the lie by claiming he'd won another £50,000. He was arrested and ordered to pay everything back. With no income, it was the people he'd duped who were probably waiting a long time.

NATIVE AMERICAN TRIBES APPARENTLY HELD REGULAR DICE GAMES AND BET ALL THEIR POSSESSIONS ON THEM

Car Crash

William Crapo Durant, Billy to his friends (and probably Crap-head to his enemies) founded automobile giants General Motors and Chevrolet, and built up a massive $120 million fortune off the back of it. He was hit hard by the Great Depression though and eventually forced into bankruptcy. If that didn't drive him spare, his final years spent managing a bowling alley probably did.

Birthday Thriller

The average birthday party consists of copious quantities of ice-cream and jelly, and a game of musical chairs. Or if you're a bit older, copious quantities of alcohol and a game of not-so-musical toilets. But for his fiftieth in 1996, the Sultan of Brunei rolled out what was reputedly the costliest birthday celebration ever. Like many parties it featured a clown with a funny nose performing, except this one was Michael Jackson, flown in to play a set at great expense. The final tab for the birthday boy's special bash was a reported $27 million. Let's hope he got some good presents out of it.

Aussie Woes

A high-rolling gambling addict is suing a Melbourne casino for large losses which occurred during a 14-month spree that ended in 2006. The man alleges that the casino attempted to lure him back to play while he was banned from every gambling house in Australia. He lost a total of AUD$36 million in a long-running baccarat marathon, or to put it another way, he was seriously down under.

Money Can't Buy Divorce

It's safe to say that Denise Reid's father wasn't a massive fan of her husband. When the wealthy man died, his will spelled out his dislike. She would only receive the £200,000 share of his £625,000 estate if she got divorced and "married someone else." Or anyone else, judging by the tone of the will. She chose love, and the money went to her brothers instead.

Band Aid

Bert Ambrose was a famous bandleader in the 1930s, but also a serious gambler. He claimed to have lost over a million in casinos over the course of 40 years. Having learnt the hard way that the house always wins, Bert invested some of his money in a West End gambling club in the early 1960s. The house didn't win in that instance though, and the club was forced to close soon afterwards due to accepting some £20,000 worth of dud cheques.

THE OPPOSING SIDES OF DICE ALWAYS ADD UP TO MAKE SEVEN

You've Been Ad

Advert sales across all media are in decline due to the effects of the recession but the Ad.com domain name still managed to fetch $1.4 million in April 2009. Surprisingly the purchaser meant to spend that much money on the domain and didn't, as you might expect, do so after accidentally clicking on a flashing web banner while attempting to remove fluff from the underside of his mouse.

Fannie Mae Not

Fannie Mae is the rather oddly named American mortgage giant set up by the government which has been predictably hard hit by the housing market crisis. It reported a $23 billion loss in the first quarter of 2009. As the saying goes, from the sub-prime to the ridiculous.

Cheating Device

In 1905, an Englishman invented a contraption he felt would help him to win big at Monte Carlo. Such devices were allowed, provided they were checked over by the casino authorities first. The man began to play roulette, entering the winning numbers into his machine, and betting based on its suggestions. He won handsomely for the first three days, but then lost the lot. His device probably didn't make it past the first bin on the way out.

3.6 MILLION UK DRIVERS WERE PENALISED WITH PARKING FINES IN 2008

No Smoke Without Litter

Smoking can damage your health and wallet, especially if you're the man from northern England who got spotted littering a cigarette butt by the authorities. He was issued an £80 penalty, but didn't pay it, and was back in court where he was further fined and had to pay costs to the tune of £565. He could have bought a rare Cuban Cohiba Behike cigar for that sort of money, and had change to buy a gold plated Zippo to light it with.

Gone to the Dogs

A greyhound trainer got into gambling in a big way, and not just on the dogs. He would regularly make up to 20 wagers a day, at £30,000 a time, and in 2006 placed a £347,000 bet on America winning the Ryder Cup (that's one way to make watching golf interesting). They lost. In an effort to stop gambling, he asked his local bookmaker (and some others) to ban him for his own good, but they allegedly let him open another account and carry on betting. Having frittered away just under £2.1 million, he decided to take the bookie to court, on the basis they'd made it too easy for him to gamble. Unsurprisingly, he lost. And had to pay costs. Still don't feel too sorry for him – dog trainers are made of money (well the Nikes my neighbour bought his poodle certainly should be, they cost him a fortune).

Born Loeser

Between October 1902 and January 1904, one Mr. David Cohn lost $10,000 betting on horses through Cincinnati bookmaker, John Payne. The gambler himself had no complaint, but M Loeser of New York decided to take action on his behalf. Despite having not lost any money himself, or being a creditor of Cohn's, or having any claim on the cash at all, he attempted to make use of a Kentucky law which allowed any third party to file a suit for three times the lost sum, provided the gambler himself hadn't already claimed. The outcome of the case isn't known, but it's highly unlikely the judge backed a Loeser.

Morning Ugly

William Hogarth produced a series of paintings in 1736 called Four Times of the Day. Morning, Noon, Evening and Night showed four very different comic views of life in London. In Morning he included an image of a woman thought to be a friend or relative who had promised to bequeath him a large sum of money. However, the portrait was slightly too realistic, and not in the slightest bit flattering. The mortified woman changed her will soon after its unveiling.

m In His Finances

on, inventor of (amongst other things) the Dual bagless vacuum cleaner, saw a drop in his fortunes of £2.0 million in 2009, according to the *Sunday Times* Rich List. Like his famous creation, that loss must really suck.

Cut Off

John Wayne Bobbitt hit the headlines in 1993 when his wife Lorena dismembered his member with a carving knife, drove to a field in her car, and threw the bloody penis out of the window. Relenting, she called 911 and after a search the item was located and packed in ice. A surgeon carefully reattached it (somehow resisting the urge to sew it onto John Wayne's forehead), and luckily, because the team didn't dick about or blow the job, the penis turned out to be nearly as good as new afterwards. Bobbitt struggled with mounting medical bills (and struggled with mounting other things no doubt) and was forced to declare bankruptcy. He did manage to earn some cash afterwards though by appearing in two porn films – *John Wayne Bobbitt: Uncut* and *John Wayne Bobbitt's Frankenpenis*. You have to feel sorry for the poor girls in those movies though. Stuck with a dead end job.

Freddie's Revenge

Freddie Mac is Fannie Mae's twin company, and also posted a 2009 substantial first quarter loss of $10 billion. Not so much a Mac daddy as an embarrassing one. Dancing at a wedding disco, possibly.

Heart Attack

In 1982, following the success of the Godfather movies and *Apocalypse Now*, director Francis Ford Coppola decided it was time to try his hand at something simpler and lighter. A cheap, self-financed $2 million musical called *One from the Heart*. Costs spiralled though, and $25 million dollars later he'd produced a box office stinker that would have been better renamed One from the Arse. He filed for bankruptcy shortly after.

You Were Done

Fred and Peter Done, owners of UK bookmakers Betfred, saw their wealth drop by an estimated £130 million in 2009 (according to the *Sunday Times* Rich List). Bet Fred never saw that coming.

A SURVEY DETERMINED THAT 22% OF LAS VEGAS GAMBLERS ARE SENIOR CITIZENS AGED 65+

Art Attack

Rembrandt was a famous seventeenth century Dutch painter whose works these days fetch millions. Even while he was alive they were very popular and he made a good living from selling his paintings, drawings and etchings. He lived well beyond his means though, frequently spending money he didn't have on art he liked and he wasn't averse to bidding up his own work either. In 1656 he'd painted himself into a financial corner and was forced to sell most of his art collection and his house (which presumably could also be classed as art, if he'd painted the walls himself).

Age No Boundaries

Playboy model Anna Nicole Smith had some money of her own, but it was nothing compared to her husband's wealth. Texas Oil tycoon J. Howard Marshall was worth a staggering $1.6 billion when they married in 1994. She was 26 and he was 89. Money might not be able to buy you love, but who cares when it can rent you a blonde topless model 63 years your junior? When Marshall died a little over a year later (who'd have thought he'd have lasted that long?), Smith probably expected a decent financial payout. What she got was an $830,000 sexual harassment suit from a former employee (a woman), which led her to file for bankruptcy in 1996, and a lengthy court case with Marshall's son that rumbled on for over a decade. The fight for Marshall's millions was still going on when Smith died of a prescription drug overdose in 2007.

RESEARCHERS IN AUSTRALIA CLAIM THAT A THIRD OF THE MONEY PUT INTO POKER MACHINES COMES FROM GAMBLING ADDICTS

Bunch of Cowboys

William F. "Buffalo Bill" Cody was a massive celebrity in the late Nineteenth and early twentieth century. Buffalo Bill's Wild West Show was a huge success and he made a sizeable personal fortune from touring it around the world. Unfortunately, Bill spent most of his money on dubious and disastrous investment schemes that never paid off. Money management clearly wasn't his strong suit (that would be the suede one with tassels on). He even managed to lose the Wild West show itself to creditors at one point. He died in 1917, most of his great fortune gone, and was buried on Lookout Mountain. Ironic as he totally failed to lookout for crap business deals while still alive.

Funking Hell

One of Funk's best-known stars had a career beset with legal problems, and in the early 1980s he signed away the rights to many of the songs he'd written. He filed for bankruptcy, but because he failed to declare those songs as a possible source of future income, a judge later ruled that he had no right to profit from them. It's estimated he lost out on tens of millions of dollars as a result. The funking idiot.

Never the Twain

Mark Twain made a fortune from his novels, including The Adventures of Huckleberry Finn and The Adventures of Tom Sawyer. He had a weakness for new technology though, and ploughed much of his earnings into inventions that never caught on (or, in some cases, never worked properly). He also launched his own publishing house which, after a promising start, collapsed and forced him to file for bankruptcy. Guess you'd call that a Twain crash.

Portfoolios

Portfolio, Condé Nast's glossy business magazine, first appeared on the newsstands in 2007. The company reportedly poured $100 million into its launch only for the title to close a mere two years later. Another bad business story for the magazine to report... If it was still going of course.

Canine Co-Star

"What is it Lassie? Tommy Rettig, the actor who played Jeff Miller in the 1950s series alongside you was trapped in financial hell? Struggled to find work after leaving the show and got into drugs and went bankrupt? Sadly died of a heart attack aged 54? Clever dog. Want a bone?"

Family Misfortune #4

Persuaded by his nephew, an American man invested $25,000 in a company that claimed to trade bank debt overseas and promised investors a 10% monthly return. Sure enough, the first month he received a payment for $2,200. He promptly invested another $83,000. The following month, instead of a cheque he received a letter from the Securities and Exchange Commission telling him that he'd been caught up in an alleged $24.5 million con and that his money was gone for good. It's safe to assume his nephew is off the Christmas card list.

Heartbreak Hotel

In the 80s, a singer purchased a share of a big hotel casino in Las Vegas. Shortly afterwards, the NBC television network alleged that he had asked the mafia to help with death threats against his family, and had been given a share of the hotel in payment. This report rubbed him up the wrong way, and he sued for libel. He won and was awarded around $20 million in damages, which were later reduced and then overturned. In 1992 he filed for bankruptcy with an estimated $20 million debt. I guess the house doesn't always win...

Amp Burns Out

Amp'd Mobile was a Mobile Virtual Network Operator (a company that provides a mobile phone service but leases its radio frequency from another network operator). It targeted American teen boys with a mix of video, music and other content but discovered a little too late that a good chunk of its audience weren't paying their bills (perhaps its target audience should have been its target audience's parents). It burned through $360 million in just two years before hanging up for good.

Fine Wine Whine

A billionaire wine collector bought four bottles of vintage Bordeaux for around £250,000 in 1988. But after a team of investigators he hired looked more closely into them ("ooh look, some wine"), he launched a law suit alleging they were fakes. In 2008 a U.S. judge reportedly dismissed the case citing jurisdiction issues, but the wine fanatic is convinced he's right and is supposedly planning further action. Look, just drink the bastard things and be done with it. Or drizzle them on chips if they are indeed vinegar.

Shopping Maul

If most of your money is invested in property it's safe to assume you're going to lose a little cash when the property market collapses. Spare a thought then for the Duke of Westminster who, according to the *Sunday Times* Rich List, saw an estimated £500 million wiped off his fortune in 2009. The loss was mostly put down to the launch of a new £1 billion shopping centre in Liverpool the previous year which had opened with a good quarter of its shops still empty. Don't feel too sorry for the not-so poor Duke though. He's still worth an estimated £6.5 billion.

Shafted

PriveCo paid $1 million for the vibrators.com domain name in November 2008. Business must really be buzzing. Either that or the seller saw them coming.

Five Grand Shuffle

In a 2007 poker tournament, three pros set up a bet amongst themselves whereby $5,000 would go to the person who managed to avoid shuffling their chips for the longest. After they sat down at the table, one asked another what counted as a chip shuffle, and the guy showed him – and of course lost out on the money. Tricked at a poker table, eh? Who'd have thought.

THE HORSE MAN O' WAR WAS VOTED THE GREATEST THOROUGHBRED OF THE FIRST HALF OF THE TWENTIETH CENTURY

Gypsy Curse

In Albania, a gypsy fortune-teller used her crystal ball to predict the stock market with unerring accuracy. She soon had thousands of investors throwing money at her and enjoying impressive returns. It all turned out to be a con though (she was paying back old investors with money from the new ones). Eventually, she declared bankruptcy and the police arrived and did a palm reading of their own involving black ink. Their prediction? A jail sentence. And that one came true.

You Gotta Have Faith

Adam Faith was an English singer, then actor, before later in his career he moved on to dabble in fiscal matters. While he was initially successful in stocks and property, his finance business eventually hit the rocks. Adam later became involved with The Money Channel on satellite TV, which turned out to be more of a money sink, closing down in 2001 and prompting Faith to declare bankruptcy, reportedly owing in the region of £32 million. As the old saying goes, first there's Faith, then hope... and we all know what comes next.

Engine Foil

A 77-year-old Filipino man was waiting for a jeepney minibus in Manila when he was approached by an old woman who said she was looking to buy a boat engine. While most people would probably have replied with "that's nice, I'm thrilled for you" and then moved as far away as possible from the crazy lady, he stayed and struck up a conversation. She opened her bag and showed him the money she was going to use to buy the engine. Two other potential passengers then joined in the conversation. Eventually, for reasons probably even he doesn't understand, the man agreed to look after the woman's large holdall of cash while the others went off looking at boat engines (which they blatantly wouldn't have been able to buy without the money). Because they said they weren't sure they trusted him, he gave them all his cash and jewellery to act as insurance until they returned. Opening the bag later he discovered it was full of newspaper and he'd been duped by a well-engineered con.

Begin Again

One source claims that a well-known poker professional once won $1 million at a poker game, then went straight over to the blackjack where he started playing every spot on the highest stakes table. Until he'd lost the lot. The definition of easy come, easy go.

From Castle To Cottage

In the 1870s, a wealthy landowner paid £6,000 for a 30 bedroom castle in the Brecon Beacons. The family moved in, and for a time enjoyed some serious wealth and status. Then one night the landowner, who was well known for his drinking and gambling, ran into a serious streak of bad luck on the cards and wagered the entire family home, including its grounds and contents on a single hand. He lost. The victor took control of the property immediately and the entire family had to leave. The new landlord did show some compassion though, and allowed them all to live in a small crofter's cottage on the edge of the estate. It wasn't so much an act of generosity as rubbing salt into the wounds. Every time the ex-landowner looked out of his window he could see the massive house he'd gambled away. Still, bet it was dead cosy in the winter.

Art Fool

Antiques experts are supposed to be able to tell the difference between clever forgeries and the real thing. That's part of the job after all. One art expert certainly should have looked a little closer when he was fooled into purchasing a counterfeit painting for £20,000. It was clearly an easel mistake to make though, as his gallery allegedly managed to sell it on for a huge profit (a 300% mark-up) before the police alerted them as to its real origins.

A Well Deserved Pay Rise

A former NHS finance director used a spot of creative accountancy to make it look as if his trust's sickly debt of £10 million was actually a healthy £1 million surplus. He took the credit for the results and was awarded a £2,500 pay rise by thrilled bosses. When it was discovered he'd exaggerated the profits he was promptly sacked, arrested and eventually jailed for 12 months. The doctored accounts are expected to make a full recovery in time.

Where There's A Will...

When a farmer died leaving behind an £18 million, 60-acre farm in Kent, his son fully expected to receive a good share of the estate. All of it perhaps, or at least most, with some going to his illegitimate half-sister. When the will was read however, he was surprised (to say the least) to hear he'd been left just £100 a year and that his sister had inherited the rest. He sued and the will was revealed to be a rather clumsy fake. It had apparently been knocked up in a word processor, the signature looked nothing like the farmer's, no one knew the witnesses, and it had been given to a sales rep for safe keeping. Despite being found out, the absence of a real will meant the sister was still entitled to receive half of the estate.

BLACKJACK WAS SO NAMED BECAUSE THE ORIGINAL GAME PAID OUT A BONUS IF THE PLAYER'S HAND CONSISTED OF THE ACE OF SPADES AND A BLACK JACK

Cry Fowl

Harry Fowler got into debt by living beyond his means. He had a large bank loan and lots of items bought on credit. Or hire purchase as it was back then in the early 1960s. His wife was apparently so stressed by the situation she left him several times. Although she was at least partially to blame for the problem as, according to Harry, she was unable to say no to the door-to-door salesmen who came calling when he wasn't at home (make of that what you will). In the end Harry filed for bankruptcy and his wife moved back home for good. She was pregnant again for the fourth time at this point so maybe it wasn't just his line of credit that needed cutting off.

Turkey Fizzler

Bernard Matthews built his fortune on turkeys. In 2009 it's estimated he lost a sizable £41 million, most of it gobbled up by the economic downturn. The controversy surrounding his popular Turkey Twizzlers (popular with children and parents, but not quite such a hit with celebrity chef Jamie Oliver) didn't help either. Matthews had already experienced a massive drop in his wealth in 2007, when an outbreak of bird flu cost him an estimated £70 million. Turkey's delight that most definitely wasn't.

Third Time Unlucky

A two-time divorcee who met her third husband over the Internet, discovered shortly before they were due to be married that he owed £20,000. She took out a loan to help him, but was not overly concerned as she knew he'd netted a £107,500 book deal. The day before his large advance payment was due he vanished, leaving her with a new £35,000 debt. She was forced to declare bankruptcy and wasn't too surprised to discover her husband's book was a work of fiction (it didn't exist). Oh, and for good measure, he was already married and had conned his other wife out of £30,000.

Taken for Granted

The *General Grant* was an American clipper ship that foundered in the Auckland Islands in 1866. It crashed into some cliffs and ended up in a cave where it eventually sank, taking with it a cargo that included 2,576 ounces of gold, worth millions at today's prices. 14 men and one woman survived and were marooned on the island for 18 long months with nothing much to keep them occupied. Well the woman and her husband probably had something to keep themselves occupied... (Bickering and blaming each other for their predicament).

From Beyond The Grave

Worried that her husband's dead first wife was haunting their home, an English woman contracted a clairvoyant to banish the spirit. He completed the task and they stayed in touch. After her husband died, things started to get really weird. Her cheque book vanished, as did thousands of pounds from her bank account. Could it be the work of a poltergeist? Then the psychic said her dead husband had been in touch, and told her to look in the back of the grandfather clock. She did so and found a will naming the clairvoyant as an equal beneficiary. She may have been gullible, but she wasn't stupid, and shortly afterwards the police came to exorcise the conman straight down to the station.

Unrefined Behaviour

In 1974, it was discovered that the UK government had paid £4 million of taxpayers' money to the sugar refineries by mistake. They had intentionally given them £33 million in subsidies to keep the prices low – an artificial sweetener, if you will – but an investigation later showed that was £7 million more than was actually needed. £3 million of the missing overpayment was later "found", leaving someone, somewhere, still in some deep sugar.

Keeping Mummy

In 1864 a case which had once contained the body of Amen-Ra, an Egyptian high priestess who had died some 3,500 years ago, was bought by a wealthy Englishman from its frankly glad-to-be-rid-of-it Arab finder. The purchaser was pleased with his bargain but lost his entire fortune a few weeks later and died shortly afterwards. A case of anything Tutankhamen can do, Amen-Ra can do better?

Funny Money

In 2005, a British man was conned out of £1,800 by two fake plain-clothed policemen. They showed him some false ID, and once inside his house explained they were investigating claims he was passing counterfeit money and asked to see all of his cash. He handed it over and was told it would be returned within an hour, but of course he never saw it again. Still, at least he had the reassurance of knowing the missing money was real.

Rolls Around

Drink driving is, of course, a very stupid thing to do. But especially if you're rich in Norway, as the fines are proportional to monthly income. As a foolish rich Norwegian found out when he was fined $30,000 for being drunk in charge of his Rolls-Royce. A liquidity loss if ever there was one.

THERE ARE THREE DIFFERENT VARIANTS OF BACCARAT, ONE OF WHICH IS BASED PURELY ON LUCK

For Richer Not Poorer

A man was swindled out of an estimated £70,000 by his own wife. She took credit cards out in his name, cashed in his life insurance, remortgaged the home and probably rootled around down the back of the settee for loose change. When caught she claimed that his children from a previous marriage were behind it all. She was arrested and jailed for two and a half years. I don't know if her husband divorced her, but it's got to be cheaper than staying married.

The Marrying Kind

One American inherited a fortune (his family was big in asbestos) but gave much of it away to ex-wives. The socialite was married 13 times, to 11 different women. His longest marriage lasted 11 years and the shortest just seven hours and 45 minutes. His final wife was a 20-year-old. Wonder what she found so appealing about the 65-year-old multi-millionaire? His madness may have had method behind it, though. It's said his trust guaranteed him a $250,000 lump sum when he married, but didn't put any limit on the number of times he could claim...

Property Cropper

If there's one place you didn't want to be invested in over the last year or so, it's property. So it's hardly surprising that one of Forbes biggest billionaire losers of 2009 was an Indian property developer by the name of Kushal Pal Singh, who reportedly lost $25 billion of his wealth, only leaving him with a "mere" $5 billion. Not so much a house price crash, as a house price six lane pile-up.

A Taylor Made Disaster

Sydney Taylor was generous to a fault. In 1958 he lent a friend £2,000, half of which was money he'd borrowed himself. The friend didn't pay it back (a friend in need is no friend take heed) so Sydney turned to gambling to try and pay off his creditors. That got him into worse debt. He sold his house and used the proceeds to gamble some more. He lost £200 on a single horse race and was £700 down by the end of the day. To make up the new shortfall he stole £700 from the company where he worked. This led to the loss of his job (after 37 years service), the loss of his pension, and a £2,000 lump sum he'd have received on his retirement. In court the judge spared him a custodial sentence, but did fine him £50, which really wasn't helping.

Spanish Gold

British ship *The Merchant Royal* sank off the coast of Cornwall in 1641. With it went a load of treasure looted from Spain including "£300,000 in silver, £100,000 in gold and as much again in jewels." Bet if the Spanish knew where it had gone down they'd have been there like a shot trying to retrieve it. They could have fished for it using their castanets.

From Sail to Fail

In 2003, round-the-world yachtswoman Tracy Edwards announced she'd secured a £38 million sponsorship package with the Gulf state of Qatar. It should have been the start of big things, but the deal capsized, and with a reported £8 million of personal debt she was sunk.

Tennis Caught

Julien Lezard was a talented tennis player who once competed in the Davis Cup. He was also an occasional jockey, a qualified barrister, and had worked for a year or so as a stockbroker. He was a bloody rubbish gambler though. In 1937, Lezard was forced to file for bankruptcy having lost £2,800 on the horses in one day and another £200 playing poker. He should have tried roulette. At least then when his luck turned bad he could have shouted "new ball please."

APPARENTLY BINGO WAS ONCE CALLED "BEANO" IN THE US, AS IT WAS PLAYED WITH DRIED BEANS USED AS MARKERS

System Addict

In 1906, a British woman came up with a foolproof way of winning at roulette. She couldn't put the idea into action herself so instead employed a team of nine men to follow her plan, paying them £7 each a week. Exactly what the system involved isn't recorded, but she lost £300 almost immediately and was forced to file for bankruptcy. She was probably forever known afterwards as the woman who became broke at the bank at Monte Carlo.

En-hard-core

In 2004, a couple at a Norwegian rock festival came on stage during a performance, and initiated a performance of their own as they shagged in front of the crowd. The band playing at the time was the Cumshots (yes, really), although this particular money shot really did cost the pair when they were reportedly fined $1,500 each for their lewd act.

High Interest

A couple took out a £5,750 fifteen-year loan to make some home improvements in 1989. Unfortunately, the company they borrowed from charged them an annual compound interest rate of 34.9% and added on various late charges and legal fees when the couple failed to make payments. By 2004 they'd paid £25,000 but still owed a further £384,000. Fortunately a judge stepped in to wipeout the outstanding amount, an act which left the couple forever in his debt.

Plate Expectations

Two businessmen went to court to decide which of them held the rights to a historic registration number made famous by motor racing legend Bill Moss. Both claimed rights to it for different reasons. The judge decided that neither of them using it would be the best bet. The stalemate cost the car enthusiasts an estimated £250,000 in legal bills. A total waste of money for something as nondescript as WTM 446. They'd have been better off scrapping over a more appropriate number plate, such as LoS3R.

Mining Disaster

Bre-X Minerals was a Canadian mining company which in 1997 reached a valuation high of $4.4 billion dollars thanks to its ownership of one of the richest gold mines ever found. It was estimated that the Busang site in Indonesia contained 70 million ounces of gold, possibly even as much as 200 million ounces. There was just one tiny problem. Hardly worth mentioning but... it was all a lie. A big, fat fib. The Busang site was largely free of the precious metal and the core samples had simply been salted with gold dust. A frenzied sell-off of shares in the fool's gold mine duly ensued, the stock collapsed and investors lost billions.

Two Chances

A woman who won an American state lottery twice – in 1985 and then again the following year – gave a large chunk of her $5.4 million winnings to friends, family and anyone who simply asked, and then gambled away the rest in an impressively short time. She had the foresight to invest the last of her remaining fortune in property though – and a very nice second-hand trailer it probably is too.

Online Addict

A compulsive gambler embezzled almost £1 million from the Scottish company he worked for to maintain his online poker habit. He stole the money over a period of three years, and appropriately enough, was jailed for three years. A pair of threes, but probably not the hand he wanted.

Premature Ending

Samuel Newburger owned a jewellery business which he sold for $100,000 in the early part of the twentieth century. He and his wife used some of the money to go travelling for a bit, but then returned to New York with a plan to increase his fortune, investing in stocks and shares. It all went wrong and eventually he ended up penniless. Unable to cope, he took his life by swallowing poison in a busy cinema. Halfway through the movie. That must have been one hell of a shit film.

THE HORSE SEABISCUIT WON 33 OF HIS 89 RACES, EARNING AROUND $430,000

Shopaholic

In 2007, a compulsive shopper was declared bankrupt after racking up debts of £250,000. She once purchased £14,000 worth of clothes and shoes (some of which didn't even fit) in a single session. What made it worse was she'd only gone out to buy a head for her electric toothbrush. Another time she went into a DIY store to buy some detergent but instead purchased 25 large tubs of UniBond because she liked the colour of the label. But we've all done that.

Refund Sought

Having lost all the money he had betting on football and playing the stock market, an unemployed American did the only thing a sane, rational man could. He packed a stun gun and a pistol and set off to kidnap the owner of the company which had given him betting advice, and demand back the $200,000 he'd gambled away. The plan went brilliantly, up to a point. He grabbed the owner and asked for his money back. George explained, not unreasonably, that he didn't have that amount of cash just lying around at home, but gave the man a $4,800 down payment and promised to hand over the rest tomorrow. He agreed – because, well, what could possibly go wrong – and drove off happy.

Unbelievably though, rather than withdrawing a massive sum of money from his bank and handing it over to a deranged loser, the owner called the police who arrested the man when he came to collect the rest of the cash the following day.

THE 7 AND 2 OFF-SUIT ARE WIDELY REGARDED AS THE WORST HOLE CARDS IN TEXAS HOLD 'EM POKER

16-to-1 Odds

Edmond Thery had a theory, and in 1897 bet Yves Guyot that within five years, by the end of 1902, 16 kilograms of silver would have the exact same value as one kilogram of gold the world over. This figure wasn't derived from intense economic research, years of studying the gold/silver price ratio or anything silly like that though. Instead it was based solely on a belief that 16/1 was a sacred ratio decreed by the laws of the universe. As it happened, by the end of 1902, the silver to gold ratio was 44/1, which could be seen as the universe sticking two fingers up to Edmond. Losing the bet wasn't all bad news though as it led to him discovering a new and incontrovertible sacred ratio: 1/53 – one idiot buys dinner for 53 friends.

Picture Imperfect

In 2006, the owner of a classic Picasso painting, was reportedly about to sell it for a colossal $139 million when he showed some friends the piece. And accidentally put his elbow through the canvas. Still, it could have been worse – he could have put his foot through it, and really, er, put his foot in it. Apparently he took the incident as a sign not to sell the painting. Or, indeed, a sign not to wave his arms around so much when he's talking. After repairs had been made, it was alleged that the painting was only worth $85 million.

Playing the Not-tery

In 1874, a clerk working in a Kentucky bookstore decided to play the lottery and purchased a ticket - number 3307. A short while later his boss received a mysterious letter from a customer called Perkins asking to buy the very same ticket having had a dream that it was the winner. The clerk wrote back and offered to sell it to him for $600. Perkins agreed. The clerk then changed his mind, and upped his request to $1,000. Again the customer agreed. By this time the clerk was so freaked out, he locked the ticket away and refused all offers. Shame then it all turned out to be a practical joke, and the ticket won nothing in the draw. Maybe he misread the number and it was really 3507. (Turn it upside down).

Party Hard

In November 2008, the Dubai resort The Atlantis staged the most expensive launch party ever seen. The star-studded champagne and lobster bash saw a colossal display of a million fireworks, with a performance from Kylie topping the bill. The cost was reported to be $20 million. They would have saved themselves a lot of money if they'd just gone with Keith Chegwin, a pair of scissors and a red ribbon.

POKER PRO CHRIS FERGUSON CAN THROW A PLAYING CARD AT 70 MPH. FAST ENOUGH TO CUT THROUGH A BANANA, APPARENTLY

Car Chase

In 1905, Mrs Ranier and Mrs Napier challenged their husbands to a race from New York to Albany. The women travelled by boat; the men by car. It should have been an easy victory for the ladies, but the men were determined and despite a long stop for lunch, and a forced tyre change, they completed the journey in six and a quarter hours – a new record. The average speed was a blisteringly fast 25 miles an hour. Fortunately for the boy racing pair there were no speed cameras about in those days.

Viva Des Moines

Poker player John Hennigan once accepted a bet that he couldn't spend six weeks living in Des Moines, Iowa (birthplace of Bill Bryson). He lost quite spectacularly, managing just two days before folding and returning bored to Las Vegas.

Whisky Galore

In 1894, William Hobby accepted a bet from Michael Hayes that he couldn't drink more whisky than any other man in the New York saloon. To win the bet (the prize is not recorded), he downed a pint of firewater in one go, then another for good measure. No horsing around for Hobby. He claimed his winnings, then set off home, but promptly died en route from drink and exposure, at least according to the report from the comically named Coroner Creamer.

No Pool like an Old Pool

The oldest death pool on record (where participants bet on people expiring) dates back to 1591. According to historians, Pope Gregory XIV had a hissy fit when he found out people were betting on his demise, and threatened to excommunicate them. Rather ironically, he passed away inside a year of declaring this edict, no doubt to the annoyance of those who had to cough up a load of money when he snuffed it.

Fishy Business

In 1896, an unnamed punter made a bet with Charles Oelrichs that he could land him like a fish. The rules of the contest were simple enough. Oelrichs would swim in the river, while the other man would try to reel him in using an ordinary fishing rod with the line fastened around the swimmer's waist. On the day of the challenge a great crowd gathered by the water to watch what the press would later refer to as the "most interesting incident of the summer" (1896 must surely have been one of the dullest years on record). It was a pretty one-sided affair, although Oelrichs did weaken briefly (or pretend to at least) but then the rod snapped and the angler conceded defeat. He wasn't entirely beaten though and the contest continued with Oelrichs' brother Hermann taking on the role of the fish, with identical results.

Shagged Pile

A Buckingham Palace footman spilled a trolley of teas on a freshly laid and very expensive carpet, according to the *Daily Mail*. It's said that some £60,000 of damage was caused, as not even professional cleaners could remove the stain, and they had to replace that section. Though why Palace staff didn't just move a coffee table over it like the rest of us would, who knows.

Stern Admonishment #2

Billionaire Joe Lewis bought up Bear Stearns shares, and lots of them. He reportedly held around 11 million, which he had paid an average of $107 per share for, when the firm collapsed in March 2008 and they became worth a fraction of that value at $10. The clue was in the name, really – he should have invested in Bull Stearns.

Mist Off

In January 2009, the *Polar Mist*, a refitted trawler carrying nearly $22 million in unrefined gold and silver (rocks with shiny bits) encountered a storm off the coast of Argentina. The crew, for reasons not entirely clear, decided to jump in the water and wait for rescue, rather than staying with their vehicle as motorists are often told to do. The ship later sank with all its precious cargo onboard. At least that's the story. Insurers Lloyds however, thought there was something rather fishy about the trawler tale and refused to pay up without proof.

Feet First

In 1895, twenty-year-old Gustav Stern made a drunken bet with a friend that he could safety jump from a moving elevated railway train onto the ground below. He succeeded in the jumping part, but failed at the safely aspect and was found at 11pm that night unconscious with a fractured skull and both feet seriously mangled after having had a close encounter with the train wheels. It's not known if his friend paid up.

The Running Man

In 1884, Paul Potter made a bet that he could run from New York's Hudnut's pharmacy to Grace church, a distance of 2 miles, in 12 minutes or less. The exact amount wagered isn't known but various parties put it at anywhere between $8 and an oddly precise $11,003.37. The run took place at 2am, and Paul approached it like a serious athlete, dressed in the latest cutting edge sports gear. Brown-checked trousers, a spotted blue shirt, a small jacket, yellow tennis shoes and a large Derby hat. He also took his own refreshments with him – a lemon, which he squeezed halfway through the run. Despite this rigorous preparation, he failed the challenge, arriving at his destination a mere 15 seconds too late. About the amount of time it takes to fish a piece of citrus fruit out of your pocket, cut it open and squeeze the juice into your mouth.

Service with a Sting

The Bugatti EB110 is a beast of a supercar with a 3.5 litre quad-turbo engine. One of these babies is worth around $500,000, so you'd think if you were a mechanic servicing it, you'd take good care of it. Either that, or take it out and give it a good thrashing before running it smack bang into a pole at speed. We all expect an inflated bill from the garage after the annual check-up, but not one to the tune of half a million.

Tim Swims

In 1894, a man identified only as "Tim" made a bet with a companion that he could swim across New York's East River. He couldn't, and promptly drowned. It's not known whether or not he handed over the money before he went into the water, but clearly his friend wasn't taking any chances as he was spotted attempting to steal $1.40 from a nearby sleeping workman the moment the challenge began. When the labourer awoke, the thief made the perfect escape by diving into the river himself, swimming along the shore and then claiming to the man who helped him out that he'd been bravely, but futilely trying to save his drowning friend.

Lampfighters

In 1901, Angelo Menzacato was stabbed in the back after a bet with James Carlavitto turned ugly. The two friends who worked as lamplighters and lived together, had wagered a sum of money on the sex of the newborn child of the King and Queen of Italy. Menzacato, who had bet that it was a boy, lost and was stabbed after failing to cough up the princely sum of $9.

Michigan Millionaire #3

A young American hit paydirt with a share of a $28 million Michigan lottery win. He received the money in annual instalments, but blew the first lot in just a couple of months. So he decided to get a businessman friend in to help manage the loot. The business "expert" advised taking a (lesser) lump sum payment instead of instalments, and assured his friend he would invest it wisely. He invested it stupidly, and blew the lot. When the winner found out what had happened, he sued his money wasting friend, and won. However, the settlement received was largely swallowed by debts and the court costs. And I expect by this time the poor lottery winner wished he'd been largely swallowed up by the Earth.

THE NAME POKER IS THOUGHT TO DERIVE FROM THE GERMAN WORD POCHEN, MEANING TO BLUFF

Bar Room Bust-up

Poker legend Johnny Moss once met a man in a bar who claimed he had never lost a fight. Perhaps thinking that he was bluffing, and spurred on by the 15-to-1 odds his friends gave him, Moss entered into a bet that he could knock the guy out. Johnny snuck up on him and delivered his best shot, which apparently wasn't good enough. Moss ended up in hospital with a collection of broken bones, and no doubt some severe bruising (to his ego).

Crusading

The lineart.com domain name sold for $13,010 in 2009. Maybe King Richard's descendents are planning a website for his birthday.

Yacht Not

Just imagine an 88-metre long super-yacht replete with every luxury you could think of, and a few more. A bit embarrassing then, if you were to prang your little sailing boat bow first into the side of it, as one skipper managed to in 2005 according to an anonymous eyewitness description. It's not known how much damage was done, but you can bet the repair bill wasn't small given that the yacht is worth $130 million or so.

BY 1910, SLOT MACHINES WERE WIDESPREAD IN THE U.S.

Rat Fan

William Henry Lewis made a $200 bet in 1883 that he could fill a barrel with 100 live rats in one hour using his bare hands. The feat was staged in a saloon bar, with tickets to watch priced at $1 each. Reports say the professional (and cheerfully pissed) rat-catcher greeted all of the spectators personally as they arrived. Things started well, but Lewis was soon covered in rat bites, including a nasty one to his mouth that wouldn't stop bleeding. With seven minutes remaining and still twenty rats to go, he admitted defeat. The audience seemed to have enjoyed watching the rats cleaving a drinking lip though, as they raised $22 afterwards to show their appreciation.

Rail Plonker #2

The warning about remembering to take all of your belongings with you when leaving the train was clearly lost on the man who left an £180,000 Goffriller violin behind. He put the instrument on the luggage rack in an effort to appear inconspicuous but then, in an effort to look like a bloody idiot, got off at the station without it. The man's insurance company put up a £10,000 reward for the violin's safe return – although I'll bet they thought it was some sort of fiddle when he first claimed.

Hedge Bet #2

The Long-Term Capital Market hedge fund got into hot water in 1998 as the Russian financial crisis of that year hit home, and the Federal Reserve was forced to organize a $3.5 billion rescue package. These hedges all seem awfully expensive. Perhaps in the future financial organisations should concern themselves with slightly smaller fry. Shrub funds, perhaps.

Copy Rat

The photocopier business isn't a particularly exciting one (not unless you've got to fix a machine at an office Christmas party). It was, however, a perfect opportunity for an American man to make some money on a con. He pretended he was an expert in the field who could buy old copiers and refurbish them, making plenty of money. He talked people into investing in his business, and reportedly fleeced them of around $130,000 in total. Not a bad haul, but compared to some of the bigger scams in this book, a bit of a pale imitation (mind you, aren't all photocopies)?

Goodness Gracious

The domain name greatfalls.com sold for $17,650 in May 2009. The seller was probably grateful for the money and the buyer no doubt really looking for greatfools.com. They're easily parted from their money, after all.

IN THE UK, UNDER-SIXTEENS CAN'T BUY A LOTTERY TICKET. NOR CAN THEY COLLECT WINNINGS FOR SOMEONE ELSE

176

The Art of Spending

One of the Saudi Sheikhs was, for a time, the greatest art buyer in the world. In one week alone he splurged £15 million on Islamic art, and it's estimated he spent a total of £1 billion over an eight-year period. He often paid way over the expected price – for instance, it's reported he spent £94,850 on an Iranian pottery tile valued at only £1,500. He was arrested in 2005, following an alleged misuse of public funds, which brought his major spending spree to an abrupt end. Auction houses around the world expressed their disappointment at no longer being able to milk the Sheikh.

Get An Ology, You're a Scientist

In the 1980s, a computer expert went bust after giving £175,000 to the Church of Scientology. £71,000 was reportedly spent on counselling and training courses ("How to waste your money" presumably being one of them). He even shelled out £15,000 for three leather bound books, autographed by church founder L. Ron Hubbard, which were described by the official receiver as being "almost worthless." Yeah, well it might look like that to the untrained eye...

SOME RESEARCHERS BELIEVE LUCK (BOTH GOOD AND BAD) COULD BE INHERITED

Mule Fool

In 1883, two men gambled over the strength of a mule. One said it could pull a sack of salt ten feet in a straight line and wagered $125 to prove it. The other, the mule's owner, said it couldn't and offered up a pair of the beasts should he turn out to be wrong. Quite why he was betting against his own animal's strength isn't known, but when the mule managed the task with ease it quickly became clear who the biggest ass there was.

Memory Marvel

Back in the eighteenth century, Daniel Hanks is reported to have made a wager with actor William Lyon that the thespian couldn't remember and recite back the entire contents of the Daily Advertiser newspaper without making a single mistake. Despite being drunk, or perhaps because of it, Lyon accepted the wager, turned up the following morning and recited the entire contents perfectly, word for word and in the exact order, jumping from editorial to adverts and back seamlessly. Hanks duly paid the bet, in the form of alcohol. It's not known if he responded to any of the adverts.

IN 1852, A MR NEILD BEQUEATHED HIS ENTIRE £500,000 FORTUNE TO QUEEN VICTORIA. NOT SURE SHE NEEDED THE MONEY REALLY

The Wheel Deal

In 1897, Conrad Heins made a bet with friends that he could ride his monowheel from New York to the Golden Gate Bridge in San Francisco in 80 days. The journey of just under 4,000 miles took him through rain storms, snow storms and sand storms and across mud plains and over mountains. Unfortunately, it also took him 83 days which meant he lost the wager. I expect he caught the train back.

Fast Food

When a restauranteur bet an acquaintance that he couldn't get married in 36 hours it must have seemed like a pretty easy bet to win. So confident was the owner of his chances that he wagered his entire restaurant. Foolishly as it happens, because his acquaintance managed to find somewhere to marry him in a nearby State and made it to the church on time. He had a ready-made place for his reception, too, in the form of his new restaurant.

Forrest Pump

A poker professional once bet $10,000 that he could bench press 225 lbs 50 times in 24 hours. He couldn't, and what's more he didn't just damage his wallet, but also his arm trying.

IN 2006, AN EDINBURGH MAN WAS REPORTED AS RACKING UP PARKING TICKETS TO THE VALUE OF £80,000

Builder's Bet

In 1935, builder Louis Revelia bet his cousin Manuel that he could swim diagonally across Central Park Lake. They cemented the deal and he dived in and set off confidently before beginning to labour. Having underestimated the job he eventually sank like a brick and drowned.

Healthy Windfall

An insurance firm gave away over £17 million to customers by accident. A decimal point error affected an estimated 140,000 policy holders, with some profiting and others losing out. The copmany allowed the lucky customers to keep the money, and compensated the unlucky ones. I'll bet that error caused a few bosses to need a check-up afterwards.

Disability Benefits

In 1961, William Day was awarded £12,500 in damages following an accident that left him disabled from the waist down. The money should have helped to make his life easier, but instead he gave it away to anyone who asked for financial assistance, including people he didn't know. He paid for one man to do his car up, bought another a motorbike so he could get to work easier, and furnished another family's home. Two years later he had no money and no friends. Lamenting his situation William Day observed "I have been a big, soft-hearted fool." A soft-headed one more like.

DESERT ORCHID WON 34 OF 70 HORSE RACES, TAKING HOME £654,000 IN TOTAL

Women Drivers

In 1903, Mrs Goode and Mrs Hoyt bet their husbands that they could drive the Hoyts' big touring car from Providence in Rhode Island to East Orange in New Jersey in one day, without any help from the men folk, and making any required repairs themselves. The men, who had achieved the same feat in reverse, agreed and sat in the back chortling as the women stalled the car several times and struggled to reach the speed required to make the distance in time (30mph). At one point a tyre exploded which "greatly frightened the women" and caused another delay as they spent ages trying to repair it. The husbands sportingly offered to extend the deadline to a day and a half or two days, which the women refused, probably with some improvised motoring hand signals. The terms of the lost wager were never disclosed but possibly involved both of them agreeing to never try that driving lark again.

Wrong in the Tooth

The NHS was conned out of £450,000 by a dentist over the best part of a decade. The man, who was jailed in 2006, made up treatments to existing clients and even "ghost" patients to siphon the cash away. Pfff. No wonder the fool got caught, everyone knows ghosts don't have teeth.

IN 2007, THE CAR NUMBER PLATE "5" WAS SOLD IN ABU DHABI FOR NEARLY $7 MILLION

Cavity Fool Insulation

In 1975, a man lost £3 million in just four months when his insulation business collapsed. Much of his wealth, most of it only on paper, had been spent on luxury living and gambling (he'd racked up losses of around £75,000) but he'd also given a large chunk of it away to friends. Sounds like his brains were woollier than his firm's loft insulation.

Good God

According to Greek mythology one of the earliest incidents of gambling was between deities Zeus, Poseidon and Hades, who cast lots for which realms they would command. Zeus got the Heavens, and Hades the underworld which wasn't so great, but still better than Poseidon who came out the big loser with the sea. Let's face it, if you wanted to be soaking wet all the time, you'd live in Manchester, where at least there are less jellyfish.

Crash Master

A well-known celebrity pranged his McLaren F1 supercar into the back of an old lady's Mini Metro back in the 1990s. The £600,000 car had its front end well and truly trashed, and it's rumoured that it cost in the order of £100,000 to fix. Perhaps he ought to have stuck to driving something cheap.

IN 2008, AN ELDERLY MAN ACCIDENTALLY REVERSED HIS CAR INTO TWO PORSCHES OUTSIDE A SHOWROOM, CAUSING DAMAGE TOTALLING £60,000

Parent Trap

An unemployed gambler borrowed heavily from his parents to pay for his habit. In 1968 his father coughed up £50,000 to settle some outstanding gambling debts, but it wasn't enough to stop the son going bankrupt. After his father died the man vowed to give up gambling for good. Back at the tables a year later he racked up a £183,900 loss, some paid for with his mother's money, the rest by loan sharks. He went bankrupt again. When asked if he'd learned his lesson this time, he said "If there is a need to gamble, I will. But it's no fun anymore." That's a no then.

A Load Of Bull

Duke de Veragua (Verruca to his friends, possibly) was a Spanish nobleman who lost his entire fortune investing in a bullring. Bull fighting was massively popular in nineteenth century Spain so building a new venue in Madrid would have been a lucrative venture. Unfortunately, he decided to invest his money in one in Paris.

Coach Capers

A tourist board spent a fortune on a luxury coach for sightseeing tours, only to discover that it was too big to fit through the city gates. Not so much a tourist bus then, as a tourist bust.

Cost of Living

In the 1960s, a baronet spent £105,000 in three years wooing a married mother of three he'd taken a shine to. For a man whose family motto was "Keep an even mind", his lack of level-headedness was impressive. He bought an expensive country house for them to live in but the household management costs proved to be cripplingly high. A short while later the bailiffs moved in, prompting the woman to move out of his life for good.

Bunny Money

In a recent domain name sale, hutch.com went for $11,770. Starsky's partner was outbid at the last minute by a suspicious looking character chewing a carrot.

Health Insurance

A Chicago couple were left on the streets when their health insurance bailed on them. When the husband was diagnosed with arthritis, excess waivers, non-deductible expenses and exempt drugs cost them a fortune. His employer, seeing lots of sick days, forced him onto a casual-labour contract – and the health insurance went with it. They filed for bankruptcy late 2008. An unhealthy loss if ever there was one.

Double Trouble

Normally, you bet on one team to win a football match. But a woman from Essex thought it would be a good idea to place two bets, for the best part of £30,000 a piece, on both sides to win when Sweden and Romania met in the 1994 World Cup quarter-final. However, she bet on the teams winning inside 90 minutes, and when the game was drawn at full-time and eventually went to penalties she lost her combined stake. Doubtless not the only time an Essex girl has rued ten men taking it in turns to step up to the box and shoot.

Save Your Love My Darling, Save Your Love

In 1932, Paul Wiener decided to marry Renee Renate. It should have been a no-brainer really. They were deeply in love and she was a model and Vienna's first-ever beauty queen. The problem was his late father's will stated that if Paul married her, his entire £500,000 fortune would be given to a Jewish charity. Sounds like Wiener envy to me.

Going Underground

The London Underground was ripped off to the tune of £5,000 by a man who repeatedly made false claims for refunds due to train delays that never happened. When he was caught, some 2,000 other such claims were discovered. That's dedication. All money down the tube, though.

IN TEXAS HOLD 'EM A PAIR OF ACES ARE KNOWN AS "POCKET ROCKETS"

For Poorer, Not Richer

In 1966, Vivien Winch married for the second time and lost £100,000. Her mother had bequeathed her the money some years previously, but only on the condition that Vivien never married again. The money was divided equally between her son and daughter who, you would like to think, bought her a good wedding gift.

B is for Beer

Sometimes attention to detail pays when listing items on eBay. As the seller of a very rare bottle of beer discovered when they spelt the name of the brew wrong. They clearly had no idea what it was worth anyway, and because of the spelling mistake it got very few views, only a couple of bids and went for $300.

The auction winner was obviously aware of the value of this nineteenth century ale, because he re-listed it – correctly spelt and with a proper detailed description – and with thousands of views the bidding went up to $500,000 (expensive for a pint even by London standards). The winning bid turned out to be a fake though, and the seller decided to keep the beer for himself, even though he reportedly received genuine six-figure bids for it afterwards. Doubtless the whole episode left the original eBayer in need of a drink, anyway.

BRITAIN'S MOST EXPENSIVE FOOD HAMPER COSTS £50,000. IT INCLUDES A £15,000 BOTTLE OF WINE. CAREFUL YOU DON'T CORK IT!

Grave Robbing

A solicitor stole some £278,000 from the estates of dead clients, filtering the cash into his own secret accounts which he used to keep his practice afloat. Eventually the business went under, he was found out, declared bankrupt, and struck off. Who says dead men tell no tales.

A Spot Of Botham

The 2009 celebrity auction at Sir Ian Botham's annual fund-raising bash reportedly included a private dinner with the cricketer. Before the bidding could begin in earnest, guests started pledging £500 a time not to have dinner with Beefy (even Botham eventually paid money to avoid eating with himself). £10,000 was quickly raised. Talent judge Piers Morgan finally matched the amount to win the "prize." Not sure what the two of them had to eat, but hopefully they didn't go out for a duck.

Baad Business

When the First World War ended, wealthy businessman Henry Fenton recognized there would be a shortage of "rags" and bought up as much stock in textile companies as he could get his hands on. It was a great idea but he got carried away and when the sheep's wool market took a dip, he lost everything.

A CHINESE AIRLINE SPENT £270,000 BUYING THE PHONE NUMBER 888-8888. SURPRISED WEIGHT WATCHERS DIDN'T BUY THAT ONE

Who Do You Owe

A British comedienne who appeared in shows such as *Who Do You Do* and *The Frankie Howerd Show* decided the best way to get more work would be to boost her profile. She bought a £9,000 Bentley, threw a celebrity banquet, stayed in five-star hotels, had her teeth fixed and shopped at Harrods. Unfortunately, the impressionist was only giving the impression of being rich – it was all on credit, and she was declared bankrupt a short while later.

Well Oiled

One of the sons of a powerfule middle-Eastern family has reportedly managed to gamble away over half a billion dollars at the tables.

Play Ball

The rare 1909 Honus Wagner card is known as the Mona Lisa of the baseball card world. Probably because he's a miserable looking git who won't crack a smile. Although some collector was most definitely smiling in 2007, when a fan paid out $2.8 million to buy it from him. Only 60 or so of the cards exist, and apparently this one is in the best condition, having been carefully wrapped and preserved in protective sheets. Yeah, yeah. I think someone else needs wrapping in protective sheets, and a nice jacket with arms that fasten up together tightly.

IN 2007, A NEWLY LAUNCHED ITALIAN SUPER-YACHT WAS RAMMED STRAIGHT INTO A HARBOUR WALL, DOUBTLESS AT GREAT EXPENSE TO THE SKIPPER

Monkey Business

Jungle.com was, for a time, the UK's second largest online retailer behind Amazon. Although it was never floated on the stock exchange, people were talking seriously of it being worth £750 million. The site made a sizeable loss in its first year however, and Argos owners Great Universal Stores swung in to buy it for just £37 million. Which made it more of a bonsai jungle, really.

Away-day Robber

A builder became a bank robber to prevent his wife discovering he owed £30,000 and was on the verge of bankruptcy. He travelled thousands of miles to London every week to commit his crimes and spent the proceeds, some £45,000, on keeping up appearances. And also on the huge train fare presumably.

Rock Bottom

Popstar PJ Proby, who once earned £1,000 a day, was banned from TV after a wardrobe malfunction (he split his trousers live on air) and was declared bankrupt in 1968. His skin tight pant-splitting antics became something of a trademark during his career. What an arse.

Property Crash

In 1985, a man was driving his new TVR 3000M down the hill to his home when the car suddenly squealed and took off full pelt. He tried to brake but the seat shot backwards and his feet could no longer reach the pedal. In a split second he weighed up the odds of the car taking off and gathering speed and chose rather to plough into the nearest wall, which happened to be his own house. He ended up in the kitchen.

It transpired that there was a fault with the accelerator pedal, or the carpet had jammed it. Luckily the guy wasn't hurt, but the £7,000 sports car was uninsured and written off. Still, it had some use even as a wreck. It was the only thing holding the house up after the accident.

Yacht Clot

A man who sold his 20-foot yacht through an online auction site made a massive gaffe when he forget to set a minimum price. It ended up going for £20 (according to reports it was worth more like £10,000). He tried to cancel the auction, but a court ruled he had to abide by its terms. The buyer certainly got the sail of the century.

RED RUM SUFFERED FROM AN INCURABLE BONE DISEASE IN HIS FOOT

The Seven-Year Pinch

A Manchester banker managed to steal £22,000 from his employer over a seven-year period. When he was finally caught in 1978 the police were at a loss as to what he'd done with the money. He lived modestly and had no vices beyond a fondness for good food. And theft.

Shelling Out

The casino always wins, but not in the credit crunch, as the economic contractions have hit Sheldon Adelson's business hard. The casino magnate was once ranked as the third wealthiest man in the world by Forbes, but his place in the billionaire charts slipped to number 15 in 2008, after he suffered estimated losses of $24 billion. What goes around the roulette wheel, comes around.

Up On The Roof

A roofer who won £60,000 on the National Lottery spent the lot on sex and drugs in just five months. Hooked on hookers and heroin he sold his house and stole from friends and family to continue fuelling his habit. Well being a roofer he was probably used to not coming down from highs.

SLOT MACHINES MAKE AROUND 70% OF THE AVERAGE CASINO'S REVENUE

Rubbery Jubbly

One Saudi businessman, once reputedly the richest man in the world, liked to take some risks with his cash. In 1986 he allegedly embarked on a nine-week roulette marathon in which his ball very much finished in the red. He lost £10 million, £3 million of which was paid by cheques that later bounced, rather embarrassingly for a billionaire. Hate to think what the bank charges were on them.

Happy Christmas

A grandmother who collected £24,000 for her local pub's Christmas club blew the lot playing roulette and then fled the country. She returned eventually but probably didn't get many Christmas cards that year.

Bending Over Backwards

Talented acrobat Francis John Merritt made a fortune after the First World War. The variety star known as The Electric Eel was, at one point in his career, earning more than the prime minister. He spent and drank it all away though (quaffing two bottles of champagne a day) and was forced to approach a circus for work. Rather appropriate, given he'd behaved like a clown.

IN TEXAS HOLD 'EM, 6 AND 9 POCKET CARDS ARE KNOWN AS A "BIG LICK." A HAND THAT REALLY SUCKS

Money Laden Bin

When a Chinese couple went on holiday, they decided to hide all the cash in their home (the equivalent of several thousand pounds) in the bin, as they figured burglars wouldn't look there. Which is true enough, but you can see where this is going. When they returned they threw the trash out, forgetting about their savings. By the time they had realized several days later, the bin bags had been collected, the money gone. All they were left with was their rubbish memories.

Get Noted

In 1937, a collection of banknotes was stolen in what police described as the perfect crime. The 70,000 notes had a face value of £10 billion but were largely worthless as they couldn't be sold on the open market. Not to mention that a banknote printed on mulberry leaves by the Kublai Khan himself might just raise a few eyebrows if you tried to buy a round with it down the Cat & Fiddle.

String Invest

The Invest.com domain name sold for over $1 million in 2007. The purchaser might have been better off buying wasteyourmoney.com, seeing as it currently only leads to a page with a handful of ads on it.

Low Energy

According to Forbes, chairman of Suzlon Energy Tulsi Tanti saw his net worth fall from $3 billion to $500 million over the course of 2008. This was due to alleged reports that the company's wind turbine blades had quality issues, which caused the stock price to plunge. Engineers looked into the problems, and concluded that the answer to them, for their associates, was blowing in the wind. Well, either that or they made a $25 million commitment towards faulty blades being repaired. One of the two.

Quiz Night

A young British man managed to rack up a £9,000 phone bill after calling premium rate TV quiz shows. The bill ran to 126 pages. He'd have been better off calling sex lines – at least he'd have got some pleasure from all that finger action.

Winner's Curse

In 1964, 73-year-old Priscilla won £3,219 on the bingo – quite a haul at the time. Deciding she had no use for the money, she sweetly gave it away. Two weeks later she won again, £960 this time. She decided to keep the second amount, stating "It doesn't seem much good giving the money away if I keep on winning." She celebrated with a nice cake. Making her Priscilla queen of the dessert. Possibly.

Blew a Download

A Canadian man who used his mobile phone continually as a modem for downloading large files, thinking it was all covered by his $10 data plan, was shocked to receive a bill for $85,000. Although it was later reduced considerably he still complained that no one from the phone company had called to tell him about the charges. They probably tried but he was busy downloading at the time.

A Real Drag

Harold Birdsdall made a failed bet on the outcome of the 1929 presidential election and in November paid the forfeit. He dressed up in his wife's clothes and jewellery, got in her car, and went for a drive around the neighbourhood. His drag act might not have garnered that much attention had he not driven through a red light and been arrested. Dressed like that you'd think he would have been keen to keep well away from red light areas.

Premature Legacy

A son couldn't wait to get his hands on his inheritance so he started spending it while his mother was still alive. He stole £1.8 million from her and used the money on a lavish lifestyle for him and his wife. He burned through the cash quickly and filed for bankruptcy, causing his brother to realize what had happened, and sue him. Happy families...

A 2008 SURVEY REPORTED THAT BRITISH DENTISTS CHARGE MORE THAN ANY OTHER COUNTRY IN EUROPE

Getting All Steamed Up

Richard Trevithick built the first full-scale working railway steam locomotive in 1804 but its principal test run came about as the result of a bet. Samuel Homfray, the proprietor of the Welsh Ironworks where it was built, was enthusing about its possibilities to ironmaster Richard Crawshay. A dubious Crawshay didn't believe that the steam locomotive could haul 10 tons of iron along a tramroad for 9.75 miles, and put up 500 guineas to prove it. He lost the bet, but had to wait to find out as the train was delayed by two hours due to engineering works in the Merthyr Tydfil area. Probably.

Travelling Man

Morton Stewart was a travel agent in 1950s Birmingham. Despite not earning much, he lived the high life, spending vast sums of money on plush hotel rooms and champagne parties. Known as "The Rich Man", Morton was suspected of running a smuggling business, but the police had little evidence. When they ran an audit on his travel firm however, they discovered a large sum of money missing. Stewart went on the run, travelling from country to country, eventually settling in Australia where he made a living selling tombstones. Hopefully he got a staff discount because when he was found dead from an overdose in 1955 all he had left to his name was nine pence.

IN 2008, FAMOUS STEEL TYCOON LAKSHMI MITTAL PAID A REPORTED £117 MILLION FOR A LONDON MANSION

Roof Jump

A Californian man once bet a Canadian poker pro $100,000 that he could jump from a car roof onto a hotel awning. He managed to succeed in jumping from a car roof onto the ground, almost doing himself a mischief in the process. And straining his bank account as well as his ankle.

Roar Talent

Frederick Thompson bet Frederick Henderson $500 that he could arrange an attraction that would bring record crowds to his holiday resort. These days that might be a Gordon Ramsay cook-off, or a Vegas-style musical spectacular. In 1901, Fred's idea was to have a couple married in the lion's cage. His mane-event did draw decent crowds but not enough to win the wager.

Murder Most Horrid

When a man won $20 million on the Illinois lottery, he probably thought he had it made. And while he doubtless enjoyed the nine years he had the dosh, his story then came to a sticky end when he was kidnapped and murdered. A rather shocking tale, more so because the murderer was his own sister-in-law, whom he'd apparently been generous to with his winnings.

IN THE LAST QUARTER OF 2008, REPOSSESSIONS ROSE 92% IN THE UK, COMPARED TO THE PREVIOUS YEAR

Sport of Kings

The first recorded yacht race took place in 1661 between King Charles II and the Duke of York, with a £100 wager to make it more interesting. The king fell a long distance behind on the way out but made up some time on the way back with more favourable wind conditions. Or perhaps the Duke of York came to the shrewd conclusion that beating the king so decisively wasn't such a good idea...

Oar-some

In 1908, athlete Fred Galloway made a bet that he could ride a dam in a row boat. On the day in question hundreds of spectators gathered to watch him succeed but in the end had to content themselves with watching him go over the falls and drown smashed to pieces in the raging rapids below. A damn failure indeed.

Old Timers

Two pensioners from San Francisco were duped out of nearly $70,000 when they received bogus calls from supposed representatives of a Canadian lottery. The poor old folks were told they'd won a million, but would have to pay the taxes due in advance. So they mailed off cheques without a second thought. There's one born every minute, and apparently there's one about to die every minute, too.

BALLY PRODUCED THE FIRST ELECTRO-MECHANICAL SLOT MACHINE IN 1964. IT WAS NAMED THE "MONEY HONEY"

No Consolation

Atari launched its 64-bit games console to rival the likes of Sega and Nintendo in 1993, but the Jaguar proved to be more of a turkey. The system was difficult to program on, which put developers off, and the 15 button controller was clunky, which put players off. When the Playstation launched in 1995, the Jaguar's demise was sealed and production ceased. According to reports approximately only 125,000 units were sold, with nearly as many (100,000) still remaining in stock at the end of 1995. Presumably these found useful employment in executive offices as paperweights or doorstops.

Prints Charming

A printer borrowed £100,000 and gambled it all away. By the time he was declared bankrupt he owed over £164,000. He so needed a licence to print money.

Play Your Cards Wrong

Anurag Dikshit is the co-founder of a company that produced a highly successful online poker website. Unfortunately for him, American citizens partook of his virtual card games, and online gambling is deemed illegal there. In 2008 he pleaded guilty to violating U.S. gaming laws, and forfeited $300 million. Even though he's a billionaire, that's going to make quite a dent in the Dikshit's fortune.

THE HOUSE ADVANTAGE FOR A PROPOSITION 7 BET IN CRAPS IS 16.67%

Guineas Pig

In 1818, Mr Ogden made a 1,000 guineas to 1 bet that his opponent couldn't throw a seven ten times in a row using an ordinary pair of dice. Seeing as the odds of doing so are approximately 60,466,175 to 1, Ogden was confident. His opponent promptly threw nine in a row. Ogden offered him 470 guineas to stop at that point, but the man, feeling understandably cocky rolled the dice a final time and... threw a nine, thereby losing the bet.

Antsy Investors

Chinese investors were ripped off to the tune of almost $400 million by a man who promised them large returns on his ant breeding scheme. Yes, you read that correctly: Ant breeding. The scheme was a big con, however, and the man was sentenced to death for his financial skulduggery. Apparently ants are valuable in China, as they're used in medicines, and also as aphrodisiacs. Although I must admit, I don't fancy yours much.

Rue-lette

In the early nineteenth century, an accomplished British gambler attempted to devise a system for beating roulette. He watched the ball spin for several hours, noted the numbers that came up, then staked his money on all the ones which had yet to make an appearance. His technique was a success and he won £700 in the first hour. Unfortunately it was downhill all the way from there and within a week he'd lost the lot.

Ten to Nothing

A hospital porter who won £10 million on the Lottery in 1996 blew the lot on fast cars, flash holidays and posh houses. Not to mention investing large sums in his local football club which subsequently got into financial difficulties. Just over ten years after his win he was declared bankrupt.

England Expects

Frank England started his gambling career in 1905 with just 75 cents to his name, but had extraordinary luck and was soon worth more than $200,000. He owned fourteen houses in New York at one point, but then things started to go badly wrong and he quickly lost his fortune. Penniless, he was forced to try a new career – burglary. That didn't work out too well for Frank either, and in 1914 the jig was finally up when police arrested him (possibly while politely enquiring why he was dancing).

Good God Goodwin

RBS suffered the biggest loss in British corporate history with Fred "the Shred" Goodwin as CEO, some £24 billion. (Ready-made headline: "Goodwin makes Badloss"). Sir Fred was previously knighted for his services to the banking world, a title that many argue he clearly doesn't deserve. Goodwin came under fire for his extravagant pension settlement, and has been dubbed the "world's worst banker" by some critics. To be honest, that title is such an achievement against the exceptionally strong competition these days it probably does deserve a knighthood.

Roll Out The Barrel

When JK O'Conner backed the wrong man in the 1892 presidential election his forfeit was to wheel a barrel of apples from Utica to New York City, a journey expected to take around seventeen days. But doubtless made to seem much longer by all those comedians he met on the way who asked him "How do you like them apples?"

Big Numbers Plate #2

The most expensive license plate in English history was sold in 2006 for a reported £330,000. And that number: "M1". So not only can you get stuck on the M1 now, you can be stuck behind it as well.

LONDON WAS VOTED THE MOST EXPENSIVE CITY IN EUROPE IN A POLL OF TRAVELLERS

Football Crazy #3

According to a newspaper report, an unnamed footballer managed to squander £1 million in one night at a casino. There are only so many houses and Bentleys you can buy, obviously.

Going Round In Circles

In 1854, a man named Hughes accepted a $3,000 bet that he could walk continuously round a track for one hundred hours without stopping. He set off briskly, aided by a stick and a friend to keep him awake. He began to seriously flag on the fourth day but was kept going due to a combination of "stimulants and light whipping." Just a normal Saturday night for some of us. By Sunday he was a shambling spectacle, uncertain as to where he was at times. At 98 hours and 40 minutes he was no longer able to walk the walk, or talk the talk, but he was able to keel the keel over and lost the bet.

Startin' Over

La Toya Jackson may look like her late brother Michael, but her singing career hardly mirrored his. In 1995 she filed for bankruptcy. Perhaps she could have earned a bob or two by standing in for her brother at Madame Tussauds during his waxwork's inevitable nose repair jobs...

Life Imitating Art

Film star Randy Quaid and his wife Evi were forced to file for bankruptcy in 2000. The couple reportedly had assets of $3.4 million but debts of $3.5 million. The situation was caused by a lengthy court battle over a 1999 film starring Randy and directed by Evi. The name of the troublesome movie, ironically, was *The Debtors* – written by Cash Bartlett.

Tooth Pasted

A man who started up a company that claimed to have invented a tooth-whitening spray orchestrated one of the biggest scams in Canadian history in 2002. He got investors on board and preyed mainly on the close-knit Ismaili community (a branch of Islam), with promises that he was going to sell the company to Colgate and they would receive massive returns. Which the tooth fairy would deliver under their pillows.

Folk didn't realize the scheme was a sham until Colgate denied any knowledge of such a sale, by which time he'd made around $75 million from some 6,000 investors. Not so much a spray as a kick in the teeth for them. The scammer was jailed for fraud, which probably gave him plenty of time to work out his next scheme. Perhaps the crook unlock (which straightens crooked teeth) or the tongue tan spray (for that truly all over bronzed look).

THE WORLD'S MOST EXPENSIVE COMPUTER MOUSE IS DIAMOND STUDDED AND COSTS OVER £14,000. EEK!

Small Problems

Gary Coleman was one of the highest paid child-actors of all-time, earning a reported $100,000 per episode for his role of Arnold Jackson on *Diff'rent Strokes*. Although he built up a significant fortune it was kept in trust and by the time he was old enough to access the money, a large chunk of it had been spent. When told about the missing millions it's probably safe to say his first words on the subject weren't "Whatchu talkin' 'bout, Willis?" In 1989 he sued his adoptive parents and a former business advisor for misappropriation of funds and in 1993 was awarded $1.28 million. It didn't last long though and in 1999 he filed for personal bankruptcy. Since then he's been to court for punching a bus driver, worked as a security guard, run over an autograph hunter in a bowling alley parking lot, and campaigned to be the next governor of California. Oh, and starred in 2009 movie *Midgets Vs. Mascots*.

Arse Nil

A British man was named the "unluckiest gambler of 2008" by bookmaker William Hill. The guy put a weekly £10 accumulator bet on 14 football teams winning. One particular week he made a last minute change to his bet, replacing the team he supported, Manchester United, with Arsenal. The other 13 teams won, as did Man United, but Arsenal didn't so he lucked out. If he had stuck with his initial choice he would have scooped an £800,000 jackpot. About the same amount Rooney gets paid to tie his bootlaces before a match.

The Unsinkable Sunk

Singer and actress Debbie Reynolds, famed for *Singing in the Rain* and being Princess Leia's mum, decided to open her own hotel and casino in Las Vegas in 1994. The Debbie Reynolds Hotel and Casino, as it was inevitably called, had a Hollywood movie museum packed with the memorabilia she'd collected over the years. It was interesting, but hardly in the same league as the MGM Grand. Three years later Debbie Reynolds, who played the unsinkable Molly Brown in *The Unsinkable Molly Brown*, was sunk and filed for bankruptcy. Perhaps she should have scaled things down and gone with Princess Leia's Mum's Bar 'n' Grill.

What's Going On?

Singer Marvin Gaye built up a sizeable fortune off the back of hits such as 'I Heard It Through the Grapevine' and 'Let's Get It On'. By the late 1970s however, he was in serious financial trouble. A drug addiction, tax problems and a costly divorce all took their toll. He agreed to give a portion of the royalties from his next LP to his ex-wife as alimony and amusingly called the album *Here, My Dear*. She probably wasn't overly grateful though, as the record was a flop and Marvin was forced to file for bankruptcy shortly afterwards.

APPARENTLY IN 2008 ALBUM SALES FELL 14% IN THE U.S.

Sympathy for the Texan

In 2002, a self-made billionaire from Texas forked out to have the Rolling Stones play his 60th birthday. Just hope he was satisfied with their performance given that it reputedly cost him around $7 million to host this party.

Steeling From The Rich

Lakshmi Mittal might still be the richest man in Britain, according to the *Sunday Times* Rich List, but the steel magnate (magnet?) took a bigger hit than most when the world economy ran into problems. A steep decline in the steel market meant he lost an estimated £16.9 billion in 2009, or to put it another way, a whopping 61% of his wealth. It's not all bad news of course, as he's steel worth a weighty £10.8 billion, more than the entire GDP (Gross Domestic Product) of Bosnia and Herzegovina.

Doggone It

In 1782, a young man jumped from Battersea Bridge into the Thames, hoping to win five guineas by swimming an agreed distance upstream in a set time. He hit the water swimming but didn't get very far as a large Newfoundland dog jumped in, swam over and dragged him to the safety of the shore. The young chap was probably barking mad about it afterwards.

Afterlife Ante

Back in 2005, a 91-year-old Devon man bet £500 that he would be dead by the end of the year. He got 6-1 odds, so if he had passed away his wife would receive £3,000, which would pay the inheritance tax bill she would face. Pretty clever, really. However, he saw 2006 in and lost the bet and his stake, though it probably didn't bother him too much. After all, it would have been his funeral if he'd won it.

Riots, Like Mama Used To Make

In 1904, Joseph Geronard refused to pay up after losing a 5 cent wager on a bowling match. So incensed were the mostly Italian crowd by his lack of gamesmanship, they started a fight which quickly developed into a riot, with people being stabbed (several died), and women throwing bricks. Guess that's what you'd call a bowling brawl.

Maxwell's Hammered

Kevin Maxwell, son of media tycoon Robert, became the biggest personal bankruptcy in UK history in 1992 according to a newspaper report, owing over £400 million. So a case of like father, like son...

AN AMERICAN MUSIC PRODUCER REPUTEDLY SPENT $6 MILLION ON HIS HOME CINEMA ROOM

Wading In

In 1783, an unnamed man accepted a large wager to walk across the Thames. Rather than attempting the well-known Jesus method, he instead built his own home-made and fully untested wetsuit out of rubber with a glass visor and tubes for air. On the day in question, a large crowd gathered and watched excitedly as he waded ponderously into the river, quickly getting knee deep. They then watched somewhat less excitedly as he turned around without a word, waded back out and made to leave. The rubber chicken. Fortunately someone in the crowd threw a brick which hit him on the head, so it wasn't a total waste of a day for the spectators.

Costly Collar

The most expensive dog collar in the world is studded with multiple diamonds and is apparently valued at close to $2 million. It's certainly special, as the dog owner who wastes that much on pooch bling will doubtless also be. Anyhow, if diamonds are a girl's best friend, and dogs are man's best friend, what does that make a diamond studded dog collar? A hermaphrodite's best friend? It's all too confusing, really.

Fizzical Education

In 1889, cigar maker Max Shillak made a $5 bet that he could down two bottles of champagne without stopping. The wager was accepted and Max got to the task. Ten minutes later he keeled over and died. According to the doctor who treated him, Max's stomach was empty and so unprepared for the the fizzy carbon-dioxide loaded bubbles which killed him. He was buried a few days later. The pallbearers shook the coffin until his head shot off into the grave and then they sprayed his body contents over the mourners. Possibly.

Landsbanki Panky

Bjorgolfur Gudmundsson, the former chairman of Landsbanki, had his wealth wiped out when the Icelandic bank hit a financial iceberg and sank in 2008, according to newspaper reports. He was a large Landsbanki shareholder, and the ensuing mess effectively destroyed his own $1 billion bank balance. And he probably won't be able to keep his football team, West Ham. Although he can still keep singing the Hammer's anthem, however, with maybe a slight modification: "I'm forever blowing billions..."

A Two-Horse Race

Having saved up $175 – a large amount of money in 1904 – Mr Watkins gambled the lot on a horse race. Florham Queen for the win and Akela for a place. The race started, and Florham Queen took an easy lead with Akela just behind. Towards the end though, just as Watkins was planning what he was going to spend his winnings on, Akela bumped into the leader, knocked her clear out of the race and got disqualified for doing so. It wasn't all bad news for the unlucky punter though. At least he hadn't gambled $600 on a 10-1 horse that won but got disqualified before the winnings could be collected. Like the previous year.

Iron Mike

Back in his boxing days, Mike Tyson was a hard punching heavyweight with a taste for victory. And a taste for ear lobes, too (he bit Evander Holyfield's ear twice in the infamous "bite fight"). Throughout his career, it's thought that he earned $300 million plus, but he was bankrupt by 2003 through a combination of bad fiscal advice and impressively voracious spending. According to bankruptcy documents he splashed out a lavish $2 million on a bathtub alone. Talk about spending money like water.

ACCORDING TO ONE REPORT, NEVADA, CALIFORNIA AND ARIZONA ARE THE U.S. STATES WITH THE HIGHEST FORECLOSURE RATES

Master Climber

In 1857, Bernard McKenna accepted a hefty wager that he could climb to the very top of a schooner's mast and make it back down again. Possibly without being caught by the police seeing as the boat in question had nothing to do with him. He shimmied up the mast and reached the top without problem, but then came over all dizzy and fell headfirst onto the deck, dying instantly. Still, technically he won the bet, so it wasn't all bad news.

Swan Dive

In 1965, Sheffield Wednesday players Peter Swan, David Layne and Tony Kay bet on their own team to lose a match against Ipswich. Ipswich won 2-0, and when the authorities discovered the wagers, the hapless trio were sent to jail for four months and banned from football.

The Lottery Liar

An English painter and decorator was so desperate to win back his estranged wife that he told her he'd scooped "up to" £8.9 million on the lottery. The lie worked but sparked a massive spending spree in which he racked up debts of £37,000, borrowed a succession of expensive cars, and even made an offer on a £300,000 farmhouse. Who says you have to pay to play? The lies inevitably unravelled however, and he was jailed for three years.

How!

Sioux warrior Black Horse and his squaw made a career out of European curiosity in the late nineteenth century, travelling from country to country and putting on shows. Eventually Black Horse began to get homesick and paid a German landlord 400 marks, all the money he had, to arrange a passage home to Deadwood. The landlord did so, and the grateful Native Americans boarded their ship. It was only when they got to New York and there was no further transport booked that they realized they'd been swindled to the tune of 230 marks. Less Black Horse, more Red Bank Balance.

Persian Plonker

In 1981, a woman spotted several men removing some priceless Persian rugs from her neighbour's house. She went out and asked them what they were doing, and they replied that the carpets were being taken away for cleaning. Thinking on her feet, she went back inside, and emerged with her own Persian thread and asked them if they'd clean that too. Of course, they cleaned her and the neighbour out thoroughly when they were never seen again.

Salt Shaker

In 1870, a widow with four young children decided to make a new life in California, and headed off to The Golden State with friends. En route from Virginia, the party stopped off at Salt Lake City. While there, she was approached by a man claiming to be an official from The Church of Jesus Christ of Latter-day Saints. He explained that all visitors were legally obliged to hand over their money to him for safekeeping so she duly gave him everything she had. The Mormon and her money were never seen again. The Moron and her children were however – heading back to Virginia after discovering her travelling companions, like her money, had also disappeared.

Irish Sighs

An American man received an email from the Irish lottery stating he'd won $800,000, even though he hadn't entered the draw. He happily paid $100,000 to release his jackpot fund, and when that disappeared without a trace he finally realized it was a scam. There's something to be said for needing a license to own a computer.

Adolph Titler

In 1889, Adolph Mafay was all set for a new life in New York. After years of hard graft working in the mines of Arizona, he'd managed to scrape together a retirement fund of $10,000. Before leaving Phoenix he purchased a lottery ticket and halfway into his journey decided to check if he'd won. He saw a room with a Lottery sign and went in. The two men inside checked the number and declared him a winner. He was invited to play again. He continued playing – winning and losing, but mostly losing – until eventually he realized he'd spent $8,800. He didn't report the loss to the police but later told a friend it only occurred to him he was being robbed when he'd run out of money. Despondent at the loss, he committed suicide. Possibly only realising he was killing himself when he'd run out of life.

Pot Red

In the days before Britain went loopy for snooker, billiards was the pocket-sized ball game of choice and John Roberts Jr. the man to try and beat. As well as being a champion player, he was also involved in manufacturing billiards equipment such as tables, rests and cue knows what else. He racked up a sizeable fortune from that, much of which he invested in three bookmakers in London. It should have been a profitable enterprise, but wire tappers set up a system to delay the results (just long enough to place a last gasp bet on the winner), and by 1898 Roberts was broke. His bookmakers lost £180,000, so in the end was surprisingly like his billiard manufacturing business. It turned out a load of balls.

AMERICA'S FIRST LAW AGAINST GAMBLING WAS PASSED IN 1638

Banks a Million

A gambling addict allegedly paid for his habit by fraudulently inflating his balance and writing illegal cheques, with the help of two accomplices at a bank. In 2002, he found himself in a sticky situation: He needed to return $3 million to the account within a day, or face the music. So as any right-thinking person would, he grabbed some cash ($1 million) and headed off to the casino to try and win the money. By lunchtime he'd reached his target, but he carried on gambling, and went on to have over $8 million on the table in front of him. An incredible come-back story! Which sadly doesn't end there as he kept on playing through the entire night and proceeded to lose every cent. And then his freedom later on when he was jailed for his actions.

Savoy-fare

In 1694, the HMS *Sussex* sank in a storm off the coast of Gibraltar. It was thought to be carrying ten tons of gold coins, payment from the British government to the Duke of Savoy, an important ally in the war against France. He wasn't best pleased when it didn't turn up ("the gold's in the sunken ship" line was probably viewed as the seventeenth century equivalent of the "cheque's in the mail") and switched sides.

Viv Spender

In 1961, Viv Nicholson won £152,000 on the football pools (equivalent to about £3 million in today's money). When asked what she would do with the cash, she famously declared that she would "Spend, spend, spend!" And she did just that, living it up and being splashed across the tabloids until she had spent, spent, spent up in just a few short years. In the 1980s she appeared on the cover of a record by The Smiths: 'Heaven Knows I'm Miserable Now'.

Home Loans

The U.S. Savings and Loan crisis of 1985 involved an avalanche of bankruptcies of local bank institutions which made home loans. The government was forced to step in and bailout costs ran to an estimated $150 billion. Savings and loans? More like ravings and groans, from the taxpayer at any rate.

A-I-Gee Whizz

AIG is a behemoth insurance company. Their job: To insure people against losses. So in 2008 what did the company do? Rack up the biggest loss going, reportedly $61 billion in the last quarter of the year alone (that's about $28 million per hour). Which makes the company look rather silly. A bit like a professional bodyguard being beaten up by a ten-year-old girl having a temper tantrum. But far more expensive to the U.S. taxpayer, of course.

IN 2007, THE VALUE OF FRAUD CASES HEARD IN UK COURTS EXCEEDED £1 BILLION

A Lott of Bother

When a UK woman found a lottery ticket on the floor of her local supermarket, she thought it was her lucky day. When she discovered it was a winner worth £30,000, she knew it was her lucky year and promptly used some of the winnings to clear her debts. However, the rightful owner reported it missing to lottery operator Camelot, who froze the remaining amount of cash and called in the police. The woman and her husband were arrested and later sentenced for fraud. Forget the old saying "See a penny, pick it up, and all day long you'll have good luck." A more appropriate version might be "See a lottery ticket, pick it up, but cash it in and you'll be f**ked."

Give It Away Now #2

In 1908, a shabbily dressed man in Pittsburgh was spotted handing out $5 and $10 bills to a large crowd. He'd inherited $5,000 but wasn't interested in the money and simply wanted to give it away. He was arrested, which might seem a bit harsh, but it's possible he was scaring the public. After all, you'd probably be intimidated if a tramp ran up offering to give you a bunch of fives.

Woeful Winner

A woman won $5 million on the Canadian lottery in 1984. She made some bad investments, including an ill-fated camp-ground, and rather foolishly forgot about paying her taxes. When the IRS came knocking she had her house seized and reportedly ended up in a trailer park. The cherry on top was subsequently being accused of attempting to take out a contract on her daughter-in-law. The hitman was an undercover detective. Get the feeling karma was trying to balance something out?

A Criminal Career

Alexander Michailoff was the son of a nineteenth century Prussian merchant. On his twenty-first he inherited his father's millions, and took just three years to spend the lot. A good deal of it went on debauched living, the rest he wasted. He was frequently conned into investing in ludicrous schemes cooked up by financial advisors promising huge gains (all for themselves). When the last of his money vanished, so did his friends. He tried working for a living, but didn't really get the idea, so eventually turned to crime, starting with fraud and petty theft. Eventually the minor criminal was arrested and given two years in jail. When he came out of prison, he turned over a new leaf, and became a major criminal, running a band of professional thieves and burglars for three years until arrested again. He never made back his millions, but that's probably just as well. He'd have been Russian to spend all that money again come the revolution.

WHEN ICESAVE COLLAPSED IN 2008, OVER 200,000 UNLUCKY BRITISH SAVERS HAD MONEY BANKED WITH THEM

Home Alone

In 1920, a prominent Canadian lawyer decided to take a trip abroad for some months, leaving his affairs in the capable hands of his son. When he returned, he discovered the boy was missing, as was his entire fortune of around $210,000. His son was eventually located and admitted spending the lot. Makes having the family home trashed as a result of a house party seem pretty tame in comparison.

Hard to Swallow

According to the historian Pliny, Cleopatra is said to have made a bet with Mark Antony to impress the Roman commander. She wagered that she could host the most expensive dinner ever. Mark Antony was probably thinking rare steaks, fried eagle eggs and a giant pyramid of Ferrero Rocher that only the Egyptians could build, but Cleo had something different in mind. When they sat down to dinner, it seemed an ordinary meal. But then she took a hugely valuable pearl earring, dropped it in strong vinegar where it dissolved, and then drank it. She won the bet, but lost a bloody fortune, as the pearl was worth the equivalent of multiple millions today.

Exxon, Exxoff

In 1989, the Captain of the *Exxon Valdez* left subordinates in charge at the helm, and the tanker hit a reef which caused the infamous oil spill. The Captain was accused of being drunk at the time, then subsequently cleared of this charge. However he was convicted of negligent discharge of oil, fined $50,000 and given 1,000 hours community service. (I bet he painted a few bus shelters in that time). The spill itself wasn't by any means the biggest in history, but due to its remote Alaskan location it cost an absolute fortune to clean up. An estimated $2.5 billion, which doubtless caused some crude words to be uttered in the Exxon board room.

Newton Discovers Gravity

Julius Newton made a million on the stock market in nineteenth-century New York, but soon after moving to London found, as his namesake had some centuries previous, that what goes up must come down. Falling shares and bad stock investments meant he was soon nearly penniless. What he didn't lose in the financial markets, he frittered away on trying to woo a succession of disinterested women and was, according to reports, something of a sex pest. Perhaps every time he saw a woman, a voice inside his head commanded "Julius, seize her!"

Waiting for God

A millionaire businessman who lost his fortune in the 1920s was forced to take on a series of low-paid jobs to make ends meet and pay for the education of his five daughters. He worked in a laundry, on the docks, as a labourer and a taxi driver (not all at the same time). One day, while driving his cab he discovered one of his passengers had left a bag behind. He opened it up and was amazed to see it was stuffed with money and jewellery. He tracked down the rightful owner and returned the bag, refusing any recompense. God, he said, would reward him. Yeah, perhaps by leaving a large bag of cash in the back of his cab? Sometimes God moves in blindingly obvious ways.

Speedy Glasweggie

A Glaswegian driver was clocked doing 168mph in his Ferrari on a Spanish motorway, according to a newspaper report. A quick way to lose money, as he was fined over £3,000.

Cashing It In

Mohamed Sahinagic was Sarajevo's wealthiest man for some years in the early twentieth century, but lost his money on a series of bad investments. Down to his last gold coin, he persuaded a goldsmith to make a bullet out of it and shot himself in the head. Now there's class for you.

ttack

..tav Fuchs lived for his art. So much so, he lost interest in the cigar manufacturing business that had given him his fortune, and allowed it to go up in smoke. Figuratively at least. Plagued by money problems he killed himself, despite being surrounded by books and paintings he could have sold to easily pay off his debts, but which he couldn't bear to be without. For some reason the newspapers reporting his death all failed to go with the obvious headline - Gustav Fuchs Off.

Beeb Blooper #2

The BBC's coffers found themselves £50,000 lighter when they had to cough up after one of its programmes said that a man had been charged with car fraud. He hadn't, and received the damages and an apology as a result. Should have asked for a refund on his license fee, as well.

A Little Short

In 1992, a German computer chess manufacturer offered £400,000 to the first westerner to face Russian world champion Garry Kasparov. Nigel Short, Britain's chess grandmaster, was one game away (which he won) from saying give us a check, mate, when the company withdrew their offer, blaming east-west politics.

Banks a Million

It's not only the contestants that suffer financial losses on the *Deal or No Deal* gameshow, but also the banker himself. He often offers them far more money than is in their box. On one episode of the UK show, he paid £120,000 for a box with £750 in it. Which makes some Royal Bank of Scotland investments look astute.

No Sex Please We're Chinese

Investors who put money into a sex theme park in China were probably not too impressed when the attraction was demolished before its launch day. Apparently Love Land featured displays of naked forms and giant genitalia – exhibitionism indeed – and officials were horrified. By the prospect of the opening of a giant vagina, presumably.

Horse Remorse

In 2008, a Scottish man who made a "placepot" bet won £140, according to a report in *The Sun*. Doesn't sound bad, until you realize that all six of his horses won and didn't merely place. If he'd have spent just a pound more on all of them coming home first, he'd have scooped the best part of £120,000. Bet he was sicker than a parrot with avian flu.

THE PROFESSOR WHO DEVISED THE FIRST SET OF 6,000 NON-REPEATING NUMBERED BINGO CARDS IN 1930 LATER WENT INSANE

Sill-y Bugger

Pleased to have reached 82 years of age, and knowing beyond a shadow of doubt that he wouldn't live to see his 83rd birthday, Dr John Sill put his affairs in order and gave away all his property and money to friends and worthwhile charities. He kept back just enough cash to live on for six months. And then didn't die. Or even get in the slightest bit ill. He appealed to his friends for a little charitable assistance, a reasonable plea given they had taken his money, but they all refused to help. He celebrated his next few birthdays in the state poor house.

Affairs in Order

In 1917, clearly not fancying his chances of surviving the war, John Lampas gave everything he owned to the Red Cross – including his car, gold watch and bank contents – and then enlisted in the army. It's not known if he survived the war but, if he did, he certainly didn't have anything to come back to.

Free Health Care

Dr Isaac Detweiler made a fortune in property, and vowed to always give a portion of any future income to the church. He stuck to his word until about 12 years before his death when he began to give all of the income from his medical practice to the church or charity. He didn't keep a single penny for himself. At least that's what he told the taxman.

IN THE 1928 GRAND NATIONAL ONLY TWO HORSES FINISHED, AFTER A FALLER CAUSED A MASSIVE PILE-UP

Web Of Lies

A Belgian man befriended a woman on the Internet and sent money to help her dying mother. Their friendship continued for a while and when the mother died he also paid for her funeral. Understandably he was less than pleased when the woman turned out to be a Nigerian scammer. And a man. He found out when he started to get emails from other people caught up in the con, and then the FBI got involved. They told him they were aware of the conman and would investigate his case if he'd fund their trip to Nigeria and pay for any expenses. The man, being an idiot, agreed. In total he lost £130,000 to the woman and the FBI, both of whom, unsurprisingly, turned out to be the same person.

Up In Smoke

In the Great Depression people were fond of hiding their money under the mattress – it was perceived to be safer than putting it in a bank (just like today). Tell that to William Kress who came back to his nice little apartment one evening and found the block on fire and everything he owned, including all his life savings, turned to ash. That's what you call burning through money.

Gin Genius

Stu Ungar was one of the most acclaimed and tragic poker players of all time. He won the World Series of Poker three times, and was an even better gin rummy player (it got to the point where he was asked not to play in gin tournaments as he just scared others off). He had superb card counting skills and could memorise multiple decks.

However, what he won at cards he would spend on drugs or gamble away on sports. He allegedly frittered away $1.5 million in one weekend of sports betting, and the first time he played golf he lost $80,000 on the practice green, before he'd even reached the first tee. He died in a Las Vegas motel room aged just 45 with only a few hundred dollars on him.

Massive Admin Charge

A British man was thrilled when he received an email telling him he had won £1 million on a lottery. The fact he hadn't actually entered the draw in question, or even heard of it, didn't seem to matter to him and he promptly sent off a cheque for £10,000, as requested, to claim his winnings. He also helpfully provided his bank account details so the money could be paid straight in. When no winnings arrived he eventually called in the police. No doubt he also asked them to investigate the mysterious non-arrival of some Viagra, a Rolex and the Fountain of Youth while they were at it.

A Load of Bologna

AJ Backus, a wealthy nineteenth-century American businessman, made a wager with friends over who could eat a set amount of Bologna sausage in the quickest time. Needless to say, they'd all had a little to drink at this point. Backus was doing well, and was just about to finish the last link when he suddenly choked and, somewhat unexpectedly, died. Perhaps he should have stuck to chipolatas.

Hokie Pokies

In the second half of 2007, gamblers in the Aussie state of Victoria reportedly lost a staggering AUD$1.3 billion solely on pokies. That's a hell of a lot of money flushed away.

Let's Get Physical

An English couple who appealed twice against a speeding fine of £60 were turned down on both counts, and then hit with a bill of £15,000 for court costs. The husband, who was a physicist, claimed the speed camera was wrong because it was improperly set up on a bend, and went into scientific detail about why this would cause erroneous readings. The judge ruled against his argument. Apparently, in court it's the law of the land, not the laws of physics that matter. Though try working a gavel without gravity.

Lotto Loser

In 2005, the biggest ever unclaimed lottery jackpot in the UK, a sum of £9.4 million, went to charity instead of the winning ticket owner who presumably lost their slip. Either that or their mind. Several people attempted to claim the prize, unsurprisingly, but none could provide a convincing enough story about how their dog/washing machine/sofa had eaten the ticket. The only thing known about the non-winner was that they were from Doncaster, which makes this a story of doubly woeful bad luck.

Snow Way

In 2005, a German radio station came up with a novel competition to see who could build a snowman in the middle of summer. One group headed off and raided some snow from nearby ice caves where it lay all year round. However, the place was environmentally protected. Photographed in the act, they reportedly faced a fine of several thousand Euro. All for a snowman. They didn't even win the competition either, as a more resourceful set of folks built one quicker – from artificial snow.

Kitty Hitch

Two cats getting married? Yes, this happened in Thailand in 1996 apparently, when two Siamese kitties tied the knot (or at the very least pawed at the ball of string). And the owners actually paid out $16,000 for a grand ceremony attended by some 500 guests. Supposedly a parrot was the best man. Well, best parrot really. Bet that made for an interesting speech.

Extra Terrible

E.T. The Extra Terrestrial was one of the biggest commercial stinkers in video game history. Released on the Atari 2600 in 1982, it has been voted the worst game of all time by several magazines. Its production was rushed for a Christmas deadline, but despite this, Atari thought the weight of the movie license (which they paid a reported $20 million for) would get it selling like hot meteorites anyway. And it did shift 1.5 million units, but the trouble was they had produced 4 million, making for huge losses. What happened to the rest? Atari denied it, but it's rumoured that loads of the unsold cartridges were dumped in a New Mexico landfill. (Who says there aren't aliens buried at Roswell?)

In the Dog House

An American couple decided to sell their house, but not in the usual way. They set up a competition asking people to name their dog. The entrance fee was $100 and the prize for the winner was their house valued at $135,000. They did add a stipulation that the competition would only go ahead if they received more than 1,300 entries, which was just as well as they actually only got 150. They didn't lose their home, but they did lose the $13,000 in savings they spent advertising the idea. Not sure what they called the dog in the end. Tornado, maybe (well they nearly lost their house because of him).

Major Fraud

A former army Major netted the top prize on the UK version of *Who Wants To Be a Millionaire*, but never got to collect his winnings. Shortly after he scooped the jackpot, it was noticed by eagle-eyed (or elephant-eared) producers that an audience member, his wife, appeared to be coughing to indicate the correct answers. The couple were arrested and tried for conspiring to cheat the show. When asked if the jury found them guilty or not guilty, the foreman waited until the judge had coughed before giving his answer.

JAMIE GOLD WON THE 2006 WORLD SERIES OF POKER MAIN EVENT AND SCOOPED A RECORD $12 MILLION PRIZE

Rang Out

In 2000, the Phone People chain of mobile phone shops was worth an estimated £50 million. Orange was reportedly interested in buying it and things were looking very good for its two young owners. But the future turned out to be neither bright, nor orange. Rapid growth led to overstretched finances and eventually the Phone People's credit was cut off, forcing the chain into administration shortly after.

Way to Seg

Launched back in 2001, the Segway is an electric self-balancing scooter or "human transporter." Although people were more likely to stare at the rider as if he or she was an alien. The producers of the Segway, who according to a *USA Today* report spent $100 million on development, believed it would be a revolution in popular transport. It would, said the creator, "be to the car what the car was to the horse and buggy." It wasn't (not unless that car was the one out of the Flintstones). The Segway sold just 30,000 units in its first six years, which compared to projected first year sales of 50,000 to 100,000, doubtless made for some steep red lines on boardroom graph charts. Still, there is a niche market for the transporter, and it's used at military bases, industrial warehouses, by security personnel in underground car parks and so forth. Basically anywhere you can't be seen in public riding the thing.

at Opportunity

When a n American County Treasurer received an email from a man in Nigeria with millions to shift out of the country, he did the exact opposite of what most sensible people would do. He jumped at the opportunity. Despite his not knowing the man, despite it being the best known scam on the Internet, despite bank officials and county employees warning him it was a con, he still invested $72,500 of his own money, and $186,500 from the County office where he worked. In total, $1.2 million went missing (no-one was quite sure where the rest ended up). He was eventually sentenced to 9 to 14 years for embezzlement. And hopefully ordered to take an email awareness course.

Fur's Not Fur

Oskar Schindler, famous for his list which saved the lives of many Jewish workers, ended his life penniless. After the war he attempted to rebuild his fortune in various ways. At one point he started an otter fur business, but the animals he bought turned out to be coypu instead. So that venture was an otter failure. He was reportedly a womaniser and an alcoholic. People who saw him drinking were no doubt pleased to be able to observe, uh-oh, Schindler's pissed.

Caught in a Trap

A council worker whose job involved logging takings from pay-and-display car park machines managed to siphon off £600,000 (in £1 coins), and spent the lot on Elvis memorabilia. She was eventually arrested and sentenced to three years in prison where, no doubt, she mastered the jailhouse rock.

Not In The Blacks

In May 2009, outdoor goods retailer Blacks Leisure reported a pre-tax loss of £6.8 million for the year to the end of February. Still, if the recession gathers more momentum trade might ironically pick up, what with all those folks now finding themselves living in tent cities...

GeoShitties

Yahoo paid a staggering $3.56 billion for GeoCities back in 1999. The web hosting site was, at the time, the third most visited destination on the Internet behind AOL and Yahoo itself. However, despite its popularity it was haemorrhaging money, having lost around $20 million the previous year. Yahoo obviously felt they could turn that around, but it never really happened and the shite-builder (home to many of the worst sites on the web) was quietly shut down in 2009.

IN 2008, THERE WERE 179,000 CASES OF ILLEGAL GAMBLING REPORTED IN CHINA

Wigging Out

In 1771, two Irish wig makers, Marsden and Cook, made a wager in a Dublin bar as to which of them could drink the most whisky. According to (probably unreliable) reports they started off with a quart, then a pint and finally a noggin. Marsden suddenly keeled over and was pronounced dead but later came back to life in his coffin, asking for a drink (methinks somebody had a problem). A surgeon was called and bled him. Unsurprisingly that didn't help. Marsden died three days later and Cook followed shortly afterwards, meaning in the end they both lost comprehensively.

Poor Decision

It quickly became clear to Allan Williams that the band he was managing was never going to hit the big time. They were nice enough lads, but a little lacking in talent, so he told them that he didn't want to be their manager any more. When a chap called Brian asked about taking over, Williams advised him not to touch them with a bargepole. Wonder whatever happened to that band, the Beatles?

TOP TEN

This section highlights, in easy, bite-sized chunks, even more tales of financial woe. From the biggest amounts ever lost in casinos to the worst people ever hired, we've included a bit of everything: bet you can't guess what the biggest dotcom disaster was!

TOP 10 RIDICULOUS GAMBLING SUPERSTITIONS

10. Some folks believe that it's bad luck to whistle when at the gambling tables. To be fair, there's some truth in this one. Not because it's unlucky, but simply because it's bloody annoying and will probably get you punched in the face.

9. The four of clubs is known as the "devil's bedstead" and is believed to be a very unlucky card that should be discarded immediately. Though that rather depends on whether it's part of a straight club flush or not.

8. Some poker players believe that taking fruit to the table brings you good fortune. Poker professional Johnny Chan started this one off by carrying a lucky orange to his games. The lemon.

7. Some card players believe that tilting your chair and twisting it three times will change your luck if you're on a losing streak. Or indeed turning your chair around and sitting on it so you're facing the seat back. Of course, that's bound to succeed. In making you look like some sort of total loser who thinks he's playing cards in a gangster movie.

6. The Chinese have a number of odd and colourful gambling superstitions. They believe that wearing red underwear brings you luck, and that if women are on their period, that is also a positive influence (although maybe that comes back to the red underwear again). It is considered lucky to urinate before a game (well, it certainly wouldn't be lucky to urinate while you're playing). Finally, the Chinese think you shouldn't have sex before gambling. Presumably because you're about to get screwed by the casino anyway.

5. Another oriental one, this time from the wonderful furniture re-arranging world of Feng Shui. Practitioners of the art claim that you should not enter a casino through the front or main door as that's unlucky. So try climbing in through a window, or descending on a wire from a skylight, preferably wearing your lucky black balaclava.

4. There are those who believe that it's really unfortunate to gamble with a dog near the table. Seems a bit odd, I've always found attractive women are more likely to distract you from the game. Just kidding... the dogs in question are of course canines, and this superstition is the inspiration for those clichéd paintings of poker playing mutts.

3. Some fruit machine players think it brings them good luck to twist their hair every time before they spin the reels. Sounds like an easy way to get a very dodgy perm to me.

2. A common but unhygienic belief is that wearing a dirty piece of clothing will bring you gambling prosperity. Not only is this rather daft, it's blatantly asking to be taken to the cleaners.

1. RABBIT, RABBIT...
Many gamblers like to carry a rabbit's foot on their key chains or wear one on a necklace to bring them luck. There are several possible theories on the origins of this old superstition. The most popular is that the rabbit is a symbol of fertility, and therefore growth and prosperity. Though if you want fertility why not just turn up at the tables with a great big severed donkey cock swinging around your neck? There is also a folk magic "hoodoo" belief that to be properly lucky, the foot in question must be the left rear taken from a rabbit shot in a graveyard by a cross-eyed man (!) at night. Lucky? The existence of such an item would be f**king miraculous more like.

A WOMAN WHO COMMITTED A £1 MILLION BENEFIT FRAUD CLAIMED A VOODOO CURSE MADE HER DO IT

TOP 1 HORRIBLE HIRES

10. Judges are employed for their sense of justice, fairness and patience. But one judge who practiced in America seemed a little lacking in the temperament stakes in 2005, when a mobile phone rang in his court room. He demanded to know whose it was, and when nobody owned up, he jailed all 46 people at the hearing and set bail at $1,500. Perhaps he misunderstood the saying "Justice for all." At any rate, he was later sacked from his high-paying circuit job. Or to put it another way, he wigged out.

9. In the U.S. the Transportation Security Administration thoroughly screen luggage in the back rooms of airports. And quite right too. Although during 2007-08 one TSA employee was more thorough than most, not just screening the luggage but testing the contents, such as laptops, cameras, etc, at home to make doubly sure they posed no threat. He apparently tested some $200,000 worth of electronics, some of which he accidentally listed on ebay. Which funnily enough was how he got caught.

8. Don't think you're paid enough? There's an easy solution if you're an American accountant with ideas above your station. Simply write yourself some cheques from the company account, and splash it on life's essentials like plasma TVs. The lady in question stole some $250,000 from her employers, until she was caught, charged with embezzlement and jailed for the best part of six years.

7. In 2007, a company director from Scotland pleaded guilty to charges of embezzling £1 million from his boss. According to the BBC he spent the cash on expensive holidays, not to mention limousines, fancy restaurant blow-outs and champagne. Where did he think he worked? A bank?

6. In 2007, a federal immigration employee and his sister pleaded guilty to taking thousands of dollars a pop from people to arrange fake marriages and get them green cards. They were fined $1.5 million and given three years of cards themselves. (There's not much else to do in prison).

5. How about the most ridiculous excuse from presumably the most ridiculous employee ever? She called to say she wouldn't be in one morning, explaining that she had taken too hot a bath and couldn't come in to work until she had laid down to cool off. I'll bet she was in hotter water when she finally arrived at the office.

4. In 2004, a cleaner at a top British gallery caused some considerable embarrassment to the gallery when they threw part of a conceptual installation in the bin. To be fair to the cleaner though, the part in question was a bag of garbage. The artist declared his valuable contemporary piece ruined, the rest of us declared him an idiot, and the whole episode is proof positive that modern art really is rubbish.

3. In 2001, Manchester United spent £28 million on Argentinian midfielder Juan Sebastien Veron, the most expensive transfer in English football at the time. He adjusted poorly to the English game and was a huge disappointment. Two years later they flogged him on to Chelsea for just £15 million (and they were lucky to get that).

2. In 1998, the San Diego Chargers, an American football team, made what is widely regarded as one of the worst NFL signings ever with quarterback Ryan Leaf. A promising college player, the Chargers forked out $31 million for his four year contract, including a record rookie signing bonus of $11.25 million. Leaf got off to a shaky start, throwing only 2 touchdowns and 13 interceptions in 9 games of his first season before being benched. He was then injured much of the time, and was released after just three years with only 4 wins to his name as a starter. Not so much a Charger as a power-cut.

1. WE ARE NOT AMUSED

The Queen may well have regretted decorating Windsor
Castle in 1992, as it's alleged that the likely cause of the
infamous fire of that year was a halogen lamp being
used too close to a curtain. The resulting impromptu
black-ash finish to the whole place gave rise to an
estimated £37 million repair bill.

THERE ARE THOUGHT TO BE AROUND 13,000 PACHINKO (PINBALL/VIDEO SLOT MACHINES)
PARLOURS IN JAPAN

TOP 10 FICTIONAL FORTUNE LOSSES

10. In the movie *Honeymoon in Vegas*, Nicholas Cage's character manages to get cheated out of $65,000 playing poker, and then puts his wife-to-be up for rental for a weekend to get out of the debt. God knows what he did for his stag night.

9. In the original 1960 *Ocean's Eleven* movie, the massive wads of cash the crooks stole from Vegas casinos ends up hidden in a coffin. Which gets cremated. Cashes to ashes, amen.

8. The banker villain of *Casino Royale*, Le Chiffre, is a real loser in this film. First-off Bond foiled his plot to blow up an airplane, evaporating a fortune the bad guy had invested in short selling the manufacturer. Then he lost multiple millions to Bond at poker, which left him royally screwed.

THE JAPANESE PACHINKO INDUSTRY IS WORTH AROUND $230 BILLION A YEAR

7. Mr Monopoly, the mascot of the famous board game, must have lost a shed load of cash over the last couple of years. The property crash surely wiped millions off his boards worldwide, with Mayfair and Boardwalk not nearly worth what they once were. Hopefully none of his mortgages were "liar loans" otherwise he'll be needing that get-out-of-jail-free card.

6. In the *Fall and Rise of Reginald Perrin*, Reggie built up a hugely successful chain of Grot shops which sold rubbish things at inflated prices. However, he abandoned his lucrative business empire after he tired of it, faking his own death once again and heading off merrily to become a tramp.

5. A fiscal farce occurs in *The Simpsons* when it's revealed that scheming nuclear plant owner Mr Burns has a $1 trillion bill in his possession. When the government come after it, he flees to Cuba and loses the note when Fidel Castro asks to look at it, then pockets it.

4. The gold bullion heist in *The Italian Job* goes like a dream, until right at the end when the lads' getaway bus skids onto the edge of a cliff, and ends up hanging in the balance with the precious metal at the back. A literal cliffhanger of an ending, but the assumption is they're stuffed. Michael Caine's last line is "I've got a great idea!" Presumably to go for a nice sit down and a cup of tea.

3. At the beginning of *The Hitchhiker's Guide to the Galaxy*, the Vogons arrive in their spaceships and demolish planet Earth. Thereby vaporising a collective colossal wealth in terms of diamonds, platinum, gold, oil, some pretty fancy houses and cars, not to mention some truly terrible limericks which would have been right up their street.

2. The Emperor lost an absolute fortune in *Star Wars* when Skywalker blasted the womp-rat sized exhaust port of the Death Star and obliterated it. The moon-sized space station must have had a galaxy-sized mortgage, and one sci-fi nerd from Alberta estimated (well, made up) its worth at $15 septillion in Earth money. Translation: A shit load.

1. LOST CONFIDENCE

Oceanic Airlines is a fictional company that has been used in a number of movies and TV shows. Oceanic's planes have been hijacked, hit by lightning, crash-landed and most famously Flight 815 was knocked out of the sky by an electromagnetic pulse in *Lost*. All of which must have cost them a packet, and made it bloody difficult for them to find an insurer.

TOP 10 GAMBLING STATISTICS

10. In 2008, 10% of adults admitted to indulging in remote gambling. That means using your computer, phone or interactive TV to gamble, not taping together sixty chopsticks so you can push your chips around the roulette table from the bar.

9. 1.6% of the adult population of the U.S. are compulsive gamblers, as are 0.6% of the adult population of the UK. So it's probably fair to say that averages out at roughly 1% of people in the western world. That means the odds of a random stranger on the street being a gambling addict is 100 to 1, which with £100 staked on it would net winnings of £10,000. Roll that over into an accumulator on the favourite running in the 2:15 at Doncaster at 2 to 1, then the 50 to 1 outsider at Aintree and that'd be a cool £1 million... Back in a bit, I'm just off down the betting shop.

...e odds of tails coming up on a coin toss is, of
...urse, 50%. Which makes the inventor of the saying
"tails never fails" a complete moron.

7. 78% of men and 68% of women gamble each
year in the UK. Given that gamblers must lose on the
whole – the house always wins, as they say – this is
actual statistical proof that men are bigger losers than
women. An assertion that fat, balding middle-aged
managers in high-powered convertible sports cars have
been proving for many years.

6. The chance of winning the UK National Lottery
is approximately 0.00000007%. Which is a rather
precise definition of f**k all. It's actually just under 1
in 14 million, which sounds marginally better. Even
so, you've got more chance of accidentally farting the
theme tune to Starsky and Hutch.

5. The average divorce rate of problem gamblers is
100% more than normal non-gambling folk. Hardly
surprising really, as they get so used to splitting pairs
in blackjack.

4. In the UK 40% of all slot machines are in public
houses, and almost all pubs have a fruit machine in
the corner of the snug. If the machines were removed,
there'd be a lot of very confused alcoholic gambling
addicts soon arrested for trying to nudge the barmaid's
melons and hold the landlord's plums.

3. Apparently 65% of pathological gamblers resort to crime to feed their addiction. So the next time someone's about to steal your wallet in the street, ask them to toss you for it.

2. A recent survey in Britain found that the most popular gambling activities were the National Lottery (57% said they played), scratch-cards (20%), betting on horses (17%) and playing fruit/slot machines (14%).

1. GAMBLING NEVER PAYS
After casinos opened up in Atlantic City, the amount of crime committed in a 30-mile radius is alleged to have increased by 100%. Although what do you expect when a host of one-armed bandits move into town? Theft likely went up considerably, not to mention muggings, and incidents of people being smashed over the head by roulette wheels. Probably.

TOP 1 REASONS NOT TO TRUST THE MONEY MEN

10. An investment advisor was accused of defrauding the deaf community of millions of dollars in February 2009. He promised returns of up to 25% through trading. It's alleged that only $800,000 was invested however, and almost all that lost. Which doubtless led to some choice – and possibly wrist-straining – demonstrations of sign language.

9. A London investment broker, jailed in March 2009, told clients that his high-performing investment fund was regulated by the Financial Services Authority. In truth, it was simply a bank account he pillaged for almost £15 million.

8. In March 2009, an American man was accused of using his investment firms to milk clients (many of whom were senior citizens) of at least $17 million to support a luxury lifestyle. He promised reliable real-estate returns, and in total is alleged to have raised over $200 million from investors.

7. A Sri Lankan celebrity and financial guru became the subject of a major international manhunt after disappearing in September 2008. He is accused of defrauding thousands of Sri Lankans of their very hard-won life savings, with the total he stole put at around $84 million.

6. For over a decade an American financier is alleged to have run a fraudulent trading fund. Apparently his investors thought they had $150 million. It wasn't even $150,000. But what's a decimal point or two (or three) between friends?

5. Zhao Pengyun was sentenced to 15 years in prison by a Beijing court in March 2009. His firm promised strong returns on forestry land, but instead lumbered hapless Chinese investors with losses of an alleged $245 million.

4. In 2009, a financial advisor was charged with fraud after the funds he managed reportedly managed to lose around $350 million.

3. Nick Leeson was a Barings bank trader who set up a special account in which he hid the mounting losses he was making. He took increasingly large stock gambles until eventually the account was down some $1.3 billion in 1995. Barings was effectively bust, and Leeson went to prison.

2. A billionaire financier was accused in February 2009 of an alleged fraud of the best part of $10 billion. Which, to be honest, just isn't cricket.

1. MADE-OFF WITH MONEY
A renowned New York financier, Bernard Madoff actually ran a ponzi scheme for decades, faking investments and paying dividends with new clients' money. His scam is believed to have cost investors $50 billion or more, and he was sentenced to 150 years in jail.

TOP 10 LOSER GAMBLING QUOTES

10. "A man's gotta make at least one bet a day, else he could be walking around lucky and never know it." – Jim Jones (cult leader). Equally, he could be walking around unlucky and not know it. Unless he steps in a dog turd.

9. "They [slot machines] sit there like young courtesans, promising pleasures undreamed of, your deepest desires fulfilled, all lusts satiated." – Frank Scoblete (author). Yes, the little slots, flashing at you, tempting you with their melons, demanding you make a deposit. Nudge, nudge, wink, wink, say no more. Get a grip, Frank! Or on second thoughts, don't.

8. "I love blackjack. But I'm not addicted to gambling. I'm addicted to sitting in a semi-circle." – Mitch Hedberg (comedian). Never thought of gambling in a shape-ist sense before. Maybe roulette players are just addicted to circles. And slot machine players are just reel addicts.

THE ODDS OF BEING DEALT A PAIR OF POCKET ACES IN TEXAS HOLD 'EM ARE 221 TO 1

7. "Gambling is a principle inherent in nature." – Edmund Burke (politician). But that doesn't make it natural. Fruit grows on trees, fruit machines do not.

6. "Aces are larger than life and greater than mountains." – Mike Caro (poker player). No they aren't. The ace of spades does look a bit like a mountain, but even so, you won't find anyone boasting about climbing the North face of it. If any further card clarification is needed vis-à-vis reality, kings and queens are not real royalty, and jacks can't be used to change car tyres.

5. "The safest way to double your money is to fold it over once and put it in your pocket." – Kin Hubbard (humourist). However, if you're a man be careful not to quadruple your money, as that sort of pocket bulge will likely be unseemly. Sextupling will probably get you swiftly arrested.

4. "A Gentleman is a man who will pay his gambling debts even when he knows he has been cheated." – Leo Tolstoy (author). Tolstoy appears to confuse the terms "gentleman" and "idiot". The real difference between a gent and a working man? A gentleman won't beat up the cheater. He'll pay someone else to do it.

3. "The only bad luck for a good gambler is bad health. Any other setbacks are temporary aggravation." – Benny Binion (casino owner). That's all very well, but the problem is how do you know if you're a good gambler?

THE MOTHER OF THE 2009 GRAND NATIONAL WINNING JOCKEY REPORTEDLY ONLY BET 50 PENCE (AT 100 TO 1) ON HIM BECAUSE SHE FEARED JINXING HIM

2. "Gambling is the future on the Internet. You can only look at so many dirty pictures." – Simon Noble (Internet bookmaker). Yes, but there are sooo many dirty pictures. And you might lose a load looking at them, but at least not a load of money.

1. LIFE IN THE WHEEL WORLD
"If I had the money and the drinking capacity, I'd probably live at a roulette table and let my life go to hell." – Michael Ventura (author). If you had serious quantities of money and drink, there are probably better things you could be doing than sitting at a table watching a load of balls, my friend.

TOP 1 PHILOSOPHICAL QUOTES ABOUT BUSINESS LOSSES

10. "To open a shop is easy, to keep it open is an art." – Chinese Proverb. Especially in these hard times. Unless it's a pawnbrokers you've opened.

9. "A business that makes nothing but money is a poor business." – Henry Ford (industrialist). That may be true, but a business that makes nothing in the way of money is soon a non-existent business. Unless it's a bank of course, in which case we all get to foot the bill.

8. "An economist is an expert who will know tomorrow why the things he predicted yesterday didn't happen today." – Laurence J. Peter (author). Indeed, and by next week he'll have invented a whole new term for whatever happened (say, erm, I don't know... perhaps "credit crunch"), and will sagely profess to have seen it all coming years previously.

7. "It is difficult, but not impossible, to conduct strictly honest business." – Gandhi (spiritual leader). Although to be honest, it's difficult to conduct any sort of business if you're wearing a nappy.

6. "Business is a combination of war and sport." – Andre Maurois (author). Yeah, you say that, but when you rugby tackle the Managing Director to the meeting room floor and spear him through the guts with a leg of the flowchart board, all of a sudden you're fired.

5. "Business is like sex. When it's good, it's very, very good. When it's not so good, it's still good." – George Katona (author). And however it is, in both cases one side usually gets screwed good and proper.

4. "It's only money." – Popular Saying. Yes, but you can buy stuff with it. Lots of stuff. Also, without it you tend to end up living under a bridge in a cardboard box.

3. "Business opportunities are like buses, there's always another one coming." – Richard Branson (entrepreneur). Unfortunately, business opportunities aren't quite such huge red double-decked entities you couldn't fail to spot the back end of. And as a result they're a bit easier to miss.

2. "Business is never so healthy as when, like a chicken, it must do a certain amount of scratching for what it gets." – Henry Ford (industrialist). Unless that business happens to be prostitution, in which case a scratching is definitely not a healthy sign.

IN 2003, A CASINO WAS DOWN $40 MILLION AFTER A HIGH STAKES SLOT MACHINE PAID OUT A RECORD JACKPOT

1. 600,000 DOLLAR MAN

"I was asked if I was going to fire an employee who made a mistake that cost the company $600,000. No, I replied, I just spent $600,000 training him. Why would I want somebody to hire his experience?" – Thomas Watson (industrialist). That's a hell of a lot of training the top bankers have to go through these days.

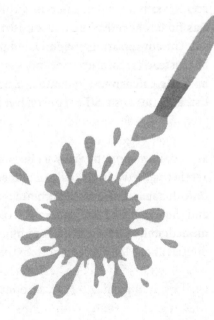

TOP 1 HIGH PROFILE JOB LOSSES

10. Revin John, a presenter on Virgin Radio Dubai, was fired for pretending to speak to God live on air. The conversation was intended to be funny, but instead (according to his bosses) simply ended up being offensive to both Muslim and Christian listeners. Jesus's traffic report never made it to air.

9. Roger Friedman was sent packing from his job as a columnist on the Fox website after reviewing *X-Men Origins: Wolverine* from an illegal leaked copy downloaded off the Internet. Fox News said they and the writer had "mutually agreed to part ways immediately" although one side might have been more mutual about the agreement than the other.

8. Prime Minister Margaret Thatcher resigned from power in 1990 due to dwindling levels of support within the Conservative party. As she left Downing Street for the last time after eleven and a half years she was pictured weeping. The British public had tears in their eyes also. Ones of joy.

7. While the majority of MPs were pretending to be profoundly remorseful/angry/embarrassed concerning the numerous ludicrous expense claims published in the *Daily Telegraph*, Commons Speaker Michael Martin felt finding and prosecuting the source of the leak should be the real focus. MPs turned on him, even though he was only really protecting their own selfish self interests and he was forced to resign (everyone loves a good scapegoat).

6. In 2008, Metropolitan commissioner Sir Ian Blair stepped down after three years as Britain's most senior policeman. London Mayor Boris Johnson had made it clear, "in a very pleasant but determined way", that he felt it was time for him to go and Sir Ian had acquiesced. In other words, Boris pulled off his Blair Ditch Project.

5. Russell Brand quit his Radio 2 show after a media storm blew up following prank phone calls he and Jonathan Ross made to *Fawlty Towers* actor Andrew Sachs. Truth be told, the loss of the job didn't really affect Russell all that much. The furore did, however, help to build further Brand awareness.

4. Lloyds Banking Group chairman Sir Victor Blank made the decision to stand down following a meeting with the board (in which, presumably, he was given little choice, although he denied that). He'd faced hostile criticism for his role in deciding to buy the troubled bank HBOS in 2008. As a parting gift he may well be given his own personalised banking stationery – I'm sure a load of Blank cheques would be very welcome.

3. Brian Clough was the legendary football manager who transformed the fortunes of three rival clubs. He took Derby County from the second division to the top of the English championship and won the European Cup with Nottingham Forest twice. With Leeds United he achieved an even more impressive feat – took them from being champions of the first division and dumped them somewhere near the bottom. A balls-up that earned him an early bath, with his contract terminated after just 44 days.

2. Judith Regan was the publisher behind the cancelled OJ Simpson project *If I Did It* – a controversial book in which Simpson described how he would have murdered his ex-wife and her friend if, indeed, he had done it. A month after the project was shelved, Regan was fired and escorted from the building.

APPARENTLY SOME AUSTRALIAN CASINOS FEATURE THE MOST BASIC GAMBLING GAME EVER: THE COIN TOSS (CALLED TWO-UP)

1. TRICKY DICKY

Richard Nixon, the 37th President of the United States, resigned from office after the Watergate scandal. He famously claimed that "There can be no whitewash at the White House", which was clearly just another lie. Without whitewash it would probably be the Mucky Yellow and Grey House.

TOP 1⬤ SONGS THAT ENCOURAGE GAMBLING

10. ABBA – 'The Winner Takes It All'. So says the Swedish pop quartet, encouraging folk to go recklessly all-in and bet their entire worth. They further recommend you should take a chance on them because it's only money, money, money.

9. Bob Seger – 'Still the Same'. Bob sang "You always won, Every time you placed a bet". A view of gambling so rosy, it's redder than half a roulette wheel. The only one who always wins in the end is the fellow taking the bets, not placing them.

8. Basement Jaxx – 'Bingo Bango'. You might think this song is just a catchy dance anthem, but it's really all about the band's love of an evening down the bingo. On a Saturday night you'll catch them all in the town hall, on the edge of their seats, with their lucky dobbers in their sweaty hands. Maybe.

IN 2006 ,86% OF SOUTH AFRICANS SURVEYED SAID THEY PARTICIPATED IN THE NATIONAL LOTTERY

7. ELO – 'Poker'. "The dream in every player's heart, To win it all, Not part, They lie awake at night". Anyone who can't sleep at night because of their gambling is in real trouble. Especially if it's the roulette wheel spinning that keeps waking them up, either that or a nudge from a casino waiter bringing them a packet of Wrigley's in lieu of brushing their teeth.

6. The Pixies – 'Dead'. Which is just what you'll be when you get home from the tables and have to tell your spouse that you've lost this month's pay cheque, maxed out your overdraft, and mortgaged your children into an Eastern European slavery ring.

5. Bob Dylan – 'Rambling, Gambling Willie'. This song tells the tale of a compulsive gambler who just can't seem to stop. And apparently with 27 children to a variety of different women, it seems like Willie couldn't stop that, either.

4. Britney Spears – 'Baby One More Time'. "Hit me baby one more time" – the theme tune of the compulsive blackjack addict who just can't say no to another card.

3. Kenny Rogers – 'The Gambler'. A classic piece of gambling advice: "You got to know when to hold 'em, Know when to fold 'em". Sadly the song neglects to mention what you've got to know when you've bet your car, house and pension on 'em, and lost 'em.

2. Elvis Presley – 'Viva Las Vegas'. The theme tune of Las Vegas which sums up the bright lights, the cacophony of excited chatter and slot machines, and that strange can't-quite-put-your-finger-on-it odour the casinos have which sort of smells like biscuits.

1. AND DON'T FORGET THE JOKER
Motorhead – 'Ace of Spades'. When Lemmy bawls out the lyrics: "You know I'm born to lose, And gambling's for fools, But that's the way I like it baby, I don't wanna live forever" it's enough to make even the most sedate of grannies hurl her knitting onto the fire and head to a backstreet gambling den, a coffee jar stuffed with her life-savings clamped under one arm, and her best set of pearl necklaces under the other.

TOP 1 BOX OFFICE BOMBS

10. Intended as the first in a franchise of action movies based around Clive Cussler's Dirk Pitt novels, *Sahara* performed reasonably at the box office, but still lost an estimated $85 million. Before its release Cussler sued a producer for failing to consult him about the script and once it had come out, probably considered suing himself for letting them make it in the first place.

9. *Zyzzyx Rd* is noteworthy for two reasons. Firstly it has a ridiculously unpronounceable name. Secondly, while it cost under $2 million dollars to make, it earned just $30 at the U.S. box office during its (very) limited release. Well, actually it made $20 as a crew member saw it with a friend and got a refund afterwards. It's probably very popular with bees though.

8. *Inchon* and *Battlefield Earth*: two religion-funded films for the price of, well, too much really. *Inchon* was produced by Rev. Sun Myung Moon and his Unification Church (aka The Moonies). *Battlefield Earth* was based on the novel by L. Ron Hubbard, founder of the Church of Scientology. Religious connections aside the films have two other things in common: they're shit and lost a ton of money.

7. The original cut of 1980's film *Heaven's Gate* was a bum-numbing five hours and 25 minutes long, trimmed to an only slightly more acceptable three hours and 39 minutes for the release (and later, in desperation, shortened again to two and a half hours). Costing $44 million, it made $3 million at the American box office and led to its studio, United Artists, being flogged off cheap to MGM. The film and the *Heaven's Gate* cult of the 1990s shared more than just the name in common. Both made you want to kill yourself once you became involved.

6. As if inflicting the Ewoks on us wasn't bad enough, George Lucas executive produced *Howard the Duck*, a tale of a talking, cigar chewing duck. The unconvincing duck suit apparently cost $2 million alone, money that might have been better invested in the script. Or in a sewage plant (still less shit). The film reputedly cost $37 million to make, and recouped just $16 million in the U.S. The duck was a turkey.

5. Kevin Costner is da bomb! Well he certainly was at the box office with *Waterworld* and *The Postman*, a pair of post-apocalypse stinkers. *Waterworld* was, at the time, the most expensive movie ever made (although it eventually recouped its budget, it initially lost money hand over fish). *The Postman* was, and remains, one of the worst films ever shat onto celluloid. Three hours of jingoistic drivel that would make any audience member think about "going postal".

4. *Ishtar* was a buddy movie starring Warren Beatty and Dustin Hoffman as two lounge singers offered a job in Morocco. But frankly no-one cares about the plot, it's all about the budget. It cost $55 million to make (a huge amount in 1987), took two years to get on the screen and thanks to negative word-of-mouth tanked worse than a Sherman.

3. *Pirates of the Caribbean* is a great film. *Cutthroat Island*, its piratey predecessor, isn't. Starring Geena Davis, the movie had an initial $65 million budget but sailed way past that to a reputed $92 million. Global earnings? $10 million. Financiers Carolco Pictures filed for bankruptcy shortly before the film came out.

2. *Town and Country* was a middle-aged romantic comedy starring Diane Keaton, Goldie Hawn and Warren Beatty. The sort of film you'd skip past immediately if you accidentally stumbled across it while channel surfing. The sort of film you certainly wouldn't expect to have the budget of a big effects-laden summer blockbuster. Cost around $105 million to make, recouped $10 million at the box office. Worldwide.

1. PLUTO CRASHED
In *The Adventures of Pluto Nash*, Eddie Murphy runs a bar. On the moon. It took 15 years for this project to get into production and once filming had finished it took another two years to get it onto the silver screen. Which was clearly a waste of someone's time and effort as hardly anybody bothered to go and watch it. Globally it made back around $9 million of its $100 million budget.

TOP 1⓪ RUBBISH GAMBLING SYSTEMS

10. Dice control. Some crap players, sorry, craps players believe that if you roll the dice in a certain way, it's possible to influence the numbers that come up. Maybe if you're Darth Vader and can use the force, yes, but us normal mortals might as well just stick to blowing on them.

9. Card counting. In fairness, card counting in blackjack – a system for keeping track of which cards have been played – works. The trouble is, casinos watch closely for card counters and will often stop them playing, or even ban them. So it's not such a great strategy in practice. I tried card counting once, but didn't win (there were 52 of them, I think).

SOME SAY THAT FRENCH MATHEMATICIAN PASCAL INVENTED THE ROULETTE WHEEL. IT WAS A BYPRODUCT OF HIS PERPETUAL MOTION EXPERIMENTS

8. Shuffle tracking. A complex technique used alongside card counting whereby you track sections of cards that you roughly know the composition of as the dealer shuffles. Basically, forget it. You'll make a total arse of it unless you happen to be a relative of Rainman.

7. Praying. A prayer to win at a casino is simply daft. If you do believe in a deity, do you really think they'll take the time out to make sure three bells come up on your next spin of the reels?

6. Labouchere system. A roulette strategy which essentially involves using a line of numbers and making bets from the sum of the end numbers. Dipping your list of numbers in the entrails of a chicken slaughtered on the night of a full moon may also help.

5. Hot tips. Often in horse racing the tipsters or a bloke down the pub will tell you about a dead cert. Just as often, however, you might as well use that other well-known high percentage method of picking a winner. Sticking a pin in the newspaper's racing page.

4. Martingale. This method involves sticking with one side of an even bet (heads on a coin toss) and doubling up your stake each time if you lose, so eventually you'll always win any lost money back plus a profit of the original stake. In theory. Trouble is, you can get some pretty long streaks of the same outcome, and the sums involved soon become astronomical. A dumb idea indeed.

PRICEWATERHOUSE COOPERS PREDICTS GLOBAL GAMBLING REVENUES WILL RISE TO ABOVE $155 BILLION IN 2012

3. Anti-martingale. Doesn't involve not using the Martingale, which would be sensible. Rather it specifies the opposite: Increase your bet after a win, and reduce after a loss. In other words, it's even more stupid than the Martingale.

2. Getting drunk. As a novice gambler nervously entering a casino for the first time, it can be all too tempting to use this unorthodox "system" to get some Dutch betting courage. Big mistake. Before you know it you'll be waking up in the gutter missing your car keys, house keys, and your shirt. The only gin rummy you should touch in a casino is the card game.

1. IT'S A BIT OF A LOTTERY
Lottery prediction programs. The chance of guessing the winning lottery numbers in the UK? 14 million to 1. The chance of getting the numbers using lottery prediction software? 14 million to 1.

TOP 1⊙ BIGGEST POP FLOPS

10. Madonna's 2003 album *American Life* allegedly sold around the 4 million mark. That's the biggest number in this Top 10, but it was still widely regarded as a commercial flop by her standards. Her previous album, *Music*, weighed in with around 11 million sales.

9. Terence Trent D'arby's first album, *Introducing the Hardline...*, was a critically acclaimed hit, chock full of funky tunes that sold an estimated 12 million records. For his second album of the 1980s, he decided to go all experimental and weird with *Neither Fish Nor Flesh*. It was surely one of the most pretentious and disappointing follow-ups ever, selling way less than the first. Although still approximately 2 million – that's a million more novelty ashtrays in the world. And a million impromptu frisbees.

8. Paris Hilton released her self-titled debut album in 2006. Fortunately, though, it mostly remained in a harmless and dormant state on shop shelves. The media branded its sales performance lacklustre, and it allegedly shifted only 75,000 copies in its first week in the States, and went downhill from there. Her record company, who apparently forked out $250,000 for the 'Stars Are Blind' video alone, weren't too impressed and went on to drop her. Stars might be blind, but unfortunately for Paris, people aren't deaf.

7. In the 1990s, Prince, or Symbol, The Artist Formerly Known as Blah-blah, Dr Wobbles or whatever name he was going under at the time, tried to make a comeback to his 'Purple Rain' days of mega-stardom. However, his 1999 album, *Rave Un2 the Joy Fantastic*, didn't leave him partying like it was that particular year when it chugged along with a relatively unimpressive 500,000 sales in the States (compared to *Purple Rain*'s estimated 13 million).

6. The Pussycat Dolls made quite an impression with their debut album *PCD*, which weighed in with something like 7 million sales. For their difficult second album (writing the band's name is probably difficult enough for the girls – perhaps the reason for the acronymed first album) they unleashed something which belongs more in the Pussycat litter tray. *Doll Domination* only managed a reported 200,000 U.S. sales in three months.

5. In 1984, Frankie Goes to Hollywood made a big (and rude) splash with the single 'Relax', followed by 'Two Tribes' (holding the UK Number 1 and 2 spots simultaneously at one stage). The following album, *Welcome to the Pleasuredome*, sold predictably well off the back of this. However, the band's second release, *Liverpool*, bombed big style. Never heard of it? Exactly. Frankie would have been lucky to get to Holyhead on the proceeds of that.

4. Robert Van Winkle's *To The Extreme*, the album that carried the hit 'Ice Ice Baby', sold multiple millions. All off that one (sampled) song. Vanilla Ice's next effort melted, as 'Mind Blowin'' was panned by critics and allegedly sold in the region of 50,000. Quite a comedown for the mal-dressed twerp with a ludicrous Mr Whippy haircut.

3. Britney's ex-hubby Kevin Federline's 2006 debut album, *Playing With Fire*, only sold around 6,000 in the first week of its U.S. release, according to one report. And dropped like a stone from there. The American public effectively delivered a slap in his face. And let's hope they do it one more time, baby.

2. Meatloaf's *Bat out of Hell* was a true monster of rock, shifting an estimated 40 million copies. However, the following albums of the 1980s weren't so good. Most notably *Blind Before I Stop*, which was more of a flaming pile of guano. It featured synth-pop keyboarding that went down like a stale loaf, and struggled to sell many copies at all.

1. GLITTER FAILS TO SPARKLE
Mariah Carey's film soundtrack album *Glitter* was released on September 11, 2001. A disastrous date for a disastrous record. According to reports, it sold over 2 million by 2002, which sounds decent enough, but isn't by her standards (*Music Box* for example has shifted something like 30 million to date). All that Glitter turned to Fritter for Carey's record company, who had to pay an alleged $28 million to end her contract early when they decided to drop her.

TOP 1**⦿** SIGNS YOU'RE A COMPULSIVE GAMBLER

10. You can't pass a fruit bowl without stopping, peering up and down at it thoughtfully, making a few tutting noises, and then attempting to nudge three grapes into a row.

9. You play snap with your nephews and end up riding away on a BMX with a Scalextric under your arm.

8. Your girlfriend suggests a romantic evening with flowers, wine, sharing a soapy bath with scented candles and then retiring to the soft silk sheets of the bedroom where you can make sweet love to round off a perfect evening. You ask what's the spread she'll give you on her legs, and bet on over six inches.

7. You change your name to Black Jack, have a roulette wheel tattooed on your back, ace of spades contact lenses, a pair of dice earrings, white silk jodhpurs, horseshoes on your footwear, you regularly chase rabbits, and have lots of money which you are often quickly parted from.

6. You can't walk across a zebra crossing without stopping to put £10 on black.

5. You realize you need help and buy one of those self-hypnosis tapes that you listen to when you sleep: "I can overcome my gambling addiction." But you still bet it won't work.

4. You're invited to stay at a friend's country house for a weekend and go out horse riding one afternoon. You put £50 on yourself and end up racing a Ford Fiesta, getting caught on a speed camera for a photo-finish.

3. You're on *Deal or No Deal* and you smash the phone to pieces. Mainly because you don't want the banker ringing up and interrupting your fun with silly pointless offers which are just slowing you down from getting to that final round.

2. After a heavy weekend at the casino you go over your overdraft limit and are summoned to see the bank manager. He tells you that you're £2,000 overdrawn. You produce a coin from your pocket and offer him double or quits.

1. FIVE-A-DAY

You claim that you have to gamble for health reasons: You get way more than your five fruit a day from the slot machines, and at 4 am in the morning there's plenty in the way of vegetables in the casino.

TOP 10 CANCELLED CELEBRITY ENDORSEMENTS

10. Tsuyoshi Kusanagi of Japanese boy band SMAP was found drunk, naked and "shrieking at the top of his voice" in a park in Tokyo in 2009. He reportedly asked the arresting officer "What's wrong with being naked?" To which the officer may have responded (but probably didn't) "Get your trousers on, you're nicked!" As a result of the scandal Toyota pulled adverts featuring the star, as did the government – he was fronting a campaign advising the public to switch to digital television. He could have advertised digital TV in the UK, having given everyone that Free view.

9. Helena Bonham Carter was signed up as the face of Yardley cosmetics in the early 1990s, a role for which she was reputedly paid £500,000. All was well until in a candid moment she said "I don't know why Yardley chose me, I don't wear much make-up." She stopped short of saying "And especially not this shit", but it was enough for Yardley to drop her.

8. Back in 2000, David Beckham didn't have golden balls, just golden curtains for hair and a slick £4 million deal with Brylcreem. Then he shaved all his locks off. As it was clear he no longer needed or could use Brylcreem on his hair the company's sales took an impressive 25% dive, but Beckham wasn't awarded a penalty.

7. Pepsi sponsored Michael Jackson for much of his career. During the filming of one of their adverts he was really on fire. Well his hair was. After he was accused of molesting a minor in 1993, he was suddenly no longer quite the hot property he'd once been and Pepsi's deal with the King of Pop went flat.

6. In 1989, Pepsi signed Madonna to a year-long $5 million endorsement contract which included rights to use her next single in a commercial. Unfortunately for them, the song was 'Like a Prayer', which had a controversial video featuring Madonna with stigmata, making love to a black saint, dancing in front of burning crosses, and so on. Under mounting pressure from the Catholic Church, Pepsi canned its sponsorship with Madonna but let her keep the money. No doubt she raised a glass or two (of Coke) to them for their generosity.

5. Hired to promote Seagram's Golden Wine Cooler products in the 1980s, Bruce Willis was dropped after getting arrested for drink driving (it's not known if the reason he lost his sponsorship was because he had the wrong brand of alcohol in his system). Shortly afterwards he decided to give up drink. Presumably he dried hard.

4. In 2008, Sharon Stone suggested the Sichuan earthquake, which claimed around 70,000 lives, could have been the result of karma for the way the Chinese have treated the people of Tibet. She was promptly dropped from Christian Dior's Chinese adverts. Karma indeed.

3. Swimming star Michael Phelps lost a lucrative endorsement deal with Kellogg's after being photographed smoking a bong. Shame he wasn't sponsored by Smack, Crackle and Pot. Interestingly, Kellogg's stock was reported to have taken a significant hit as a result of dropping Phelps for his bong toting.

2. A leading singer lost a fortune after allegedly assaulting his famous girlfriend. Aside from having to cancel numerous appearances (as did the poor woman) he also lost various lucrative sponsoring deals.

1. WHAT A SNORTY GIRL

When the *Daily Mirror* published photographs they claimed showed Kate Moss taking cocaine, everyone was shocked. It's usually *The News of the World* that breaks these kind of stories, not the *Mirror*. The public were hugely disappointed in her too. She was shown snorting through a rolled up £5 note. Surely a supermodel of her standing could easily afford to use a twenty. As a result, she lost contracts with H&M, Stella McCartney and Burberry. Chanel also said it would not be renewing its contract with her, doubtless a monetary loss that was nothing to be sniffed at.

TOP 1⦿ DOT-COM DISASTERS

10. Kibu.com, an online community for teenaged girls, held a flashy launch party in August 2000. It was the start of great things. The end of great things came just 46 days later, when the company shut up shop without even troubling to spend all of the $22 million it had raised in venture capital.

9. MVP.com sold sporting goods. Directors of the site included basketball legend Michael Jordan, Ice Hockey star Wayne Gretzky and American football quarterback John Elway. These celebrity endorsements did little for the site though as it went bust within a year. Sounds like someone fumbled the ball (not Gretzky then).

8. govWorks.com was designed as a place for ordinary citizens, businesses and local government to interact. Like any dot-com, it started, raised huge sums of money, lost huge sums of money and went bust. Unlike other similar sites its success and failure was filmed and later released as a movie – *Startup.com*.

7. Go.com was a web portal owned by the Walt Disney Company. It had its own content, but also linked to other related sites, such as Disney.com. In 2001, with visitor numbers falling, a decision was made to discontinue it. Four hundred employees were laid off and Disney took a $790 million non-cash hit.

6. InfoSpace was an advert funded alternative to Yellow Pages whose stock price reached a massive high of $1,305 a share in 2000, making it worth in excess of $31 billion (more than Boeing). Its success didn't last though. In 2002 it was worth just $2.67m.

5. theGlobe.com was a social networking site that in 1998 set a record for IPOs and was valued at over $840 million. Its founder was filmed dancing on a table in a nightclub with his model girlfriend, before announcing, "Got the girl. Got the money. When theGlobe.com crashed, he lost the girl and the money.

4. Online toy retailer eToys was valued at $8 billion at its height but its success didn't last. It went bust in 2001, found a new owner, went bust again and found another new owner.

3. Pets.com sold pet supplies online. The problem was that pets didn't shop on the web, and their owners weren't overly keen either. The site spent a reported $11.8 million on advertising but shifted just $619,000 worth of goods in its first 12 months. Pets.com lasted a little under two years.

2. Webvan was a site set up to retail fruit and veg. Initially it just sold produce locally in the San Francisco Bay Area, but then expanded to eight other U.S. locations. It secured $375 million in an IPO and it seemed the world was its carrot. But then reality chomped hard. Webvan quickly ran out of cash and ended up giving away all non-perishable stock.

1. BOO HOO

Boo.com was a web-based sports and fashion retailer with a cutting-edge website. The sort of website you wished you had a cutting edge you could use to slash your wrists while waiting for it to load. Graphics heavy, with pseudo 3D views and an animated sales assistant called Miss Boo, it took forever if you were on dial-up. Sales, like the site, were slow, and returns high – not good when Boo was paying for postage. It had over 420 people on the payroll (when it was reported just 30 would have been enough), the office was guarded by Gurkha soldiers, and the whole thing became a sob story when boo.com burned their way through $188 million in just six months.